£12·50

D0772506

OXFORD ENGLISH MONOGRAPHS

General Editors

JOHN CAREY   STEPHEN GILL

DOUGLAS GRAY

THE CAVE
OF MAKING
The Poetry of
Louis MacNeice

ROBYN MARSACK

CLARENDON PRESS · OXFORD
1982

Oxford University Press, Walton Street, Oxford OX2 6DP
London Glasgow New York Toronto
Delhi Bombay Calcutta Madras Karachi
Kuala Lumpur Singapore Hong Kong Tokyo
Nairobi Dar es Salaam Cape Town
Melbourne Auckland
and associates in
Beirut Berlin Ibadan Mexico City Nicosia

Published in the United States by
Oxford University Press, New York

British Library Cataloguing in Publication Data
Marsack, Robyn
    The cave of making. —(Oxford English monographs)
    1. MacNeice, Louis—Criticism and interpretation
    I. Title
    821'.912   PR6025.A316Z/
    ISBN 0-19-811718-3

Library of Congress Cataloging in Publication Data
Marsack, Robyn.
    The cave of making.

    (Oxford English monographs)
    Bibliography: p.
    Includes index.
    1. MacNeice, Louis, 1907-1963—Criticism and
interpretation. I. Title.
PR6025.A316Z78   821'.912   82-7844
    ISBN 0-19-811718-3

Typeset by DMB (Typesetting) Oxford
and printed in Great Britain
at the University Press, Oxford
by Eric Buckley
Printer to the University

To the Memory of
Nigel Charles Marsack
1947-1979

CONTENTS

ACKNOWLEDGEMENTS

Among those who aided my research, and to whom I am indebted, are: Dan Davin, the late Professor E. R. Dodds, Mrs T. S. Eliot, Joy Flint, Karl Gay (former Curator of the Poetry Collection at Buffalo), John Hilton, Mrs Hedli MacNeice, the late Gerald Murray, the late Lady Elizabeth Nicholson, and Jon Stallworthy. As the supervisor of the thesis on which this monograph is based, John Fuller was unfailingly helpful. My chief debt is to Nicole Jordan, for trenchant criticism which both fortified and modified my sense of what I was doing.

My thanks are due to efficient librarians of the Berg Collection, the Bodleian, the Humanities Research Centre; to Peter Croft of King's College, Cambridge, Miss Hutchings of the BBC Play Library, and Miss Reed of the BBC Script Library.

The writing of the book was made possible by generous grants and support from St. Catherine's College, the English Faculty Board, the Graduate Studies Committee, and Wolfson College, Oxford.

I am grateful to the following for kind permission to use material and to quote from copyright sources: Henry W. and Albert A. Berg Collection, the New York Public Library, Astor, Lenox, and Tilden Foundations; Professor Anthony Blunt; the BBC; the Louis MacNeice Collection, Rare Book and Manuscript Library, Columbia University, New York; Mr D. M. Davin, as MacNeice's Literary Executor; Faber and Faber; the Humanities Research Centre, University of Texas at Austin; King's College Library, Cambridge; Marlborough College, for the excerpt from the Literary Society's minutes; Edward Mendelson for the letter from Auden, which is copyright © 1979 by the Estate of W. H. Auden; the Poetry/Rare Books Collection of the University Libraries, State University of New York at Buffalo.

I. THE THIRTIES: PRIVATE FACES

It may be, as Cyril Connolly wrote, that 'the golden recipe for
Art is the ferment of an unhappy childhood working through a
noble imagination': it is certain that for Louis MacNeice his
early years in an Ulster rectory were remembered as a grim
period of incubation. There was the natural distance kept from
a minister's son, compounded by the father's political stance
at a time of radical disturbance in Ireland. Not that the family
were of Anglo-Irish stock, on the contrary its forebears on both
sides were Irish, though never the peasants MacNeice boasted
of in the 'Last Will and Testament' he composed with W. H.
Auden:

> And to my own in particular whose rooms
> Were whitewashed, small, soothed with the smoke
>   of peat,
> Looking out on the Atlantic's gleams and glooms,
>
> Of whom some lie among brambles high remote
> Above the yellow falls of Ballysodare
> Whose hands were hard with handling cart and boat
>
> I leave the credit for that which may endure
> Within myself of peasant vitality and
> Of the peasant's sense of humour...

(Letters from Iceland)

In the genealogy of heroic dimensions he constructed in a letter
to his schoolfriend Anthony Blunt, MacNeice included Con-
chobar MacNessa: ancestry marrying strength and style,
undiluted by planters' blood. John Frederick MacNeice's
position in the Church of Ireland, however, allied the family
with the Protestant Ascendancy. When MacNeice compared
his childhood to that of Yeats, one of the similarities was the
outspoken Home Rule sympathies of their fathers, whose
position was typical rather of the Catholic Irish. His sister,
Elizabeth Nicholson, justly points out that their father was
revered by his parishioners, with a real affection unaltered by
his stand against the Ulster Covenant in September 1912.

The MacNeice and Clesham families were from the west of Ireland. Mrs MacNeice in particular felt Carrickfergus to be alien territory, and talked of Connemara to her children. It became for them a dream world, where speech was soft like their father's: '... my mother spoke of it so constantly and with such love and such longing that I think it was she who really made it come alive for both Louis and myself. It became for us both a "many-coloured land", a kind of lost Atlantis where we thought by rights we should be living ...'.[1] Such tangled allegiances especially affected MacNeice. While Lady Nicholson recalls contact with children outside the rectory, for MacNeice as the youngest child the nursery was the centre, and he shared it with a brother whose mongolism was not then recognized as such. He took to school the memory of William's seeming idiocy, the more vivid because the boy had been away and the other two supposed that in the interim he had been cured, would return companionable. 'And the boys at Sherborne seemed suddenly terribly young; I had learned their language but they could not learn mine, could never breathe my darkness.'[2]

Not only was there that constant shadow, but also the death of an adored and vital mother, who had inexplicably fallen into sadness and weeping, then had left for a nursing home in Dublin in 1913, when MacNeice was five years old. The superstition already rife in the household, unknown to his father, must have coalesced with the aftermath of his mother's late obsession with the hellish aspects of religion, childhood nightmares, his father's anguished aloofness, to produce a feeling of intense, elemental isolation.

All this was thrown into relief by schooling in England: the yellow of Sherborne, the downs of Marlborough, communal rites. MacNeice recalled the contempt of the Irish for the English, 'an identification of Ireland with the spirit and of England with crass materialism'.[3] He might have been educated in Ireland but for his father's remarriage into a milieu in which it was traditional for the children to be sent away, and in his autobiography MacNeice admitted to the sense of release he experienced when Littleton Powys, headmaster of Sherborne, dismissed the Orange Day celebrations: '"Isn't it all mumbo-jumbo?" ... To be speaking man to man to Powys and giving the lie to the Red Hand of Ulster was power, was freedom, meant I was nearly grown up.'[4]

The division of experience was physically sharp: Carrick-fergus, with the rectory 'lit by oil lamps (not enough of them) ... full of shadows', church, and the cemetery across the garden hedge, little beguiling company; Sherborne, Marlborough, Oxford, with their attendant mental stimuli, gradually secure friendships, and country expeditions in spring and early summer. Of course this is too simple a map, emotional territories overlapped, there was unease on both sides of the Irish sea also pleasure on both. Nevertheless there is much truth in it. MacNeice identified certain traits in his poetry as a reaction to the fear, monotony, and loneliness he associated, however exaggeratedly, with life in Ulster: '... what I now think an ex-cessive preoccupation in my earlier verse with things dazzling, high-coloured, quick-moving, hedonistic or up-to-date.'[5]

A certain verbal flamboyance may also have been a result of his decision to exploit the fact of his Irishness at school. Powys recalled MacNeice's keeping his Sherborne dormitory en-thralled by stories, and although his youthful poems do not have a narrative cast, their rapidity of association and move-ment from one image to the next demonstrate his inventive skill.[6] Thus extravagance in speech conformed to the English stereotype of the Irish, but was also an assault on Ulster dour-ness and restrictions by a boy who increasingly cherished his western-Irish ancestry.

At Marlborough, where John Betjeman remembers him as looking like a poet, and 'always writing poems in that thick hand with those very strong uprights in the letters', MacNeice was langorously attached to Keats and Swinburne, had an odd penchant for Noyes, came under the influence of the Celtic Twilight.[7] Yet he also brought along to the Lower Sixth Literary Society poems by T. S. Eliot, as the minutes record. Mr Waring, an American master, 'kindly gave some rather necessary explanatory remarks' before 'Rhapsody on a Windy Night', 'Morning at the Window' and 'The Hollow Men' were read. The secretary noted the audience's being 'very interested by these, though we did not feel competent to pronounce any definitive judgement on their comparative methods'.[8] When MacNeice set out to describe the impact of Eliot's poetry on

his school contemporaries, who 'wanted to play Hamlet in the
shadow of the gasworks', he naturally found they had taken
from *Poems 1909-1925* what they needed to support such an
attitude.[9] There was scant appreciation of technical skill but
quick identification with Prufrock and with the atmosphere of
'Preludes', in which MacNeice 'found not only that "smell"
of a modern city which your first visit establishes as part of your
mentality, but also the human element below that surface,...
we knew in our bones, if not explicitly, that this which Eliot
expressed so succinctly and vividly, this was what we were up
against'. He accounts for the immediate appeal of 'The Hollow
Men' by adolescent preference for a dream/nightmare landscape, without instancing its influence on his own poems: 'Tomorrow falls the shadow / From Death, the broken statue;' or
'Through fields bone-tenanted, / Striated column, / Pillar
truncated'. MacNeice's idiosyncratic version of Pythagoras in
'A Lame Idyll' has clear affinities with 'Prufrock' and 'Preludes': 'While on his bald head the weary rain drips. / In the
street below bob windy bits of paper'; there is a brief imitation
of Eliot's quatrains in 'Coal and Fire'. Even when MacNeice
moved beyond the first, very artificial phase of his writing,
Eliot claimed his attention and admiration, and became one of
the few people from whom he invited criticism.

'I watched the words, / Coming to drink at my mind.'[10] This
is the impression given by the fluent juvenilia of the Marlborough and Oxford years, published by Gollancz in *Blind
Fireworks* (1929). The writing was sometimes almost automatic,
little altered after the first rush of words. It was not fake; as
MacNeice remarked of the fantastic mythological mixture
'Twilight of the Gods': 'The fault of such a poem lies not in its
feeling but in its technique.'[11] A young poet usually reads more
than he can catch up with; it is as immediately absorbing as his
everyday experience and in MacNeice's case served partly as a
defence against that. The exhilaration of literary and artistic
discovery could crowd out parts of his life that seemed in-
communicable. Voluntary abdication of control over the words
perhaps matched MacNeice's sense that events in the world
were arbitrary, and that the only way to cope with them was to
detach oneself, chronicle decay, give it mythic proportions.

When MacNeice was ready to confront his life more directly,

to move away from the demise of gods, 'corpse carousal', the universe fading in the distance, he found four components of the Ulster landscape persisting in both his work and dreams:

Sea (i.e. the grey Lough fringed with scum and old cans), fields (i.e. the very small, very green hedged fields of Northern Ireland), factories (i.e. those small factories dotted through the agricultural patchwork), and gardens (i.e. my father's medium-sized lush garden with a cemetery beyond the hawthorn hedge) ...[12]

He maintained that the place, time, and family one is born into condition the images a poet uses instinctively, and took as an example his early autobiographical poem, 'Trains in the Distance'. It is not free from the kind of outmoded poetic epithets that abound in *Blind Fireworks*; the 'smoky ribbons' rising from the trains are also described as 'full-rigged galleons', but the rooting of images in experience serves him well. Mac-Neice was not moved, as his contemporaries later were, by any sense of mechanical intrusion into a pastoral setting, nor by exultation in the power of the engines. These are almost disembodied sounds and signs of trains, they are reassuring, a physical quality conveyed by the lines' purring, 'Trains came threading quietly through my dozing childhood, / Gentle murmurs nosing ...', 'that metal murmur'. An alliterative pattern is used with enough constancy to convey the tranquillity of the summer and, because of its continuation in the last line, the fog-horn both cuts across the quiet and is made part of the pattern, alien and recurrent. 'That menace from the sea' is an early example of the fear and fascination water held for the poet, on which he dwelt to the last volume. The Lough, rarely blue, was forbidding and dangerous, yet a symbol of escape.

In *Poems* (1935), his second collection, this sometimes benign, sometimes threatening landscape was much more sharply particularized. MacNeice himself ascribed the change in his approach partly to growing up—that is, 'a) working for a salary, b) living in a large city, c) married'—and partly to reading Eliot's essays, thereby being 'diverted from anarchism'.[13] After a disturbed final year at Merton College, MacNeice had received a First in Greats in 1930, and had married Giovanna Marie Thérèse Babette Ezra, to the dismay of both their families. Mary, as she was known, was the step-daughter of Sir John Beazley, the great expert on Greek vase-painting. They left Oxford for Birmingham, where MacNeice took up a lecture-ship in Classics at the University. Establishing himself in Birmingham meant opting for English urban life, while the tug of Ireland compelled him to consider conflicting claims upon his loyalty. He later wrote of Yeats's escape from the quicksands of the nineties: 'he harnessed the aesthetic doctrine to a force outside himself which he found in his own country', and to some extent this was the saving of MacNeice's work. A new alertness to his environment radically changed both the subject-matter and form of the poems, which had been part of an essentially private fantasy world. In *Modern Poetry* (1938), where MacNeice was particularly concerned to present the poet as an ordinary man, his writing being a way of returning to normal from the 'kink or deficiency' he starts out with, he concluded his 'Case-Book' with the move to Birmingham:

> ... I realized that while it is an asset to have an idiom, an idiom is only valuable as a differentiation of what is communal. Further, I had to earn my own living and this is antipathetic to a purely aesthetic view of life. And lastly, living in ... Birmingham, I recognized that the squalor of Eliot was a romanticized squalor because treated, on the whole, rather bookishly as *décor*. (*Modern Poetry,* p. 74)

Differences in form betray differences in attitude. MacNeice was inclined to give Yeats's influence precedence in the 1930s, suggesting that Eliot's nihilism, despite some superficial resemblances, was distant from the poetry of Auden and his contemporaries, who like Yeats staked their belief on a system and on human capacity for heroic action. He considered the two most influential earlier English poets to be Blake and Donne: '...it is significant that, whereas we shared Donne with Eliot, we shared Blake with Yeats; our aim was to use our brains, ... but to follow Blake in not abjuring life or the world of "created things".'[14]

The admiration of MacNeice's generation for Yeats's later poetry was a response, as to Eliot's previously, to its 'modern-ity'. His reaction against Eliot's assumption of chaos pleased them: things should be selected and patterned, and naturally poems had a regular pattern also, while flexibility of language avoided 'poetic' diction. They appreciated the widened range of subject-matter which accorded with their own concept of poetry, 'dealing fairly directly with contemporary experience, some of it historical, some of it casual and personal'.[15]

Yet the past to which Yeats could confidently refer, particularly the splendid Anglo-Irish version of it he constructed for himself, was not a source of poetry for MacNeice. He was spurred now by his own act of seeing, and it is precisely this unencumbered, critical, occasionally still apocalyptic vision that is noticeable in the poems. Committed to living in England, MacNeice is harsh about Northern Ireland, visually and to some extent politically. There are real threats bearing out childish intuitions: in 'Belfast' (1931) and 'Turf-stacks' (1932) the community that sends the trains, and those that ignore them, or would prefer to do so, are bleakly portrayed.

At the end of the Lough now it is not merely the fog-horn that sounds out, but an industrial clamour inseparable from the two creeds that support it: that of puritan industrialists to whom 'the salt carrion water' brings wealth, and of the men who labour where 'like crucifixes the gantries stand' ('Belfast'). The violent religious imagery, the sense that like the 'harsh / Attempts at buyable beauty' the Virgin's protection is up for sale, and like the merchandise is false to its outward promise, this bitterness is a more complete denunciation of the context of his childhood than MacNeice approached in the wistful sensuousness of the poems in *Blind Fireworks*. The 'cowled and pilgrim moon' of an early poem, 'Sunset', becomes the sinisterly tangible 'country of cowled and haunted faces'. Even the syntax has a tortuousness one might connect with evangelizing rhetoric. Although MacNeice associates himself with those 'who walk in the street so buoyantly and glib', 'Belfast' has neither quality. It tends to confirm his status as being outside both the sections of society he portrays, a position made explicit in 'Turf-stacks'.

In such a poem, MacNeice comes closest to the stereotype of the thirties, praising the proletariat and prophesying the millennium. Because of his background he idealizes not the factory-worker but the peasant; that it is an idealization, perhaps a reaction against life in Birmingham, is plain in the poem's progress to the more convincing third stanza, where desperation gives a keener edge to the language than when it is employed in somewhat facile praise or contempt. The 'iron horses' are symbolic of the mechanization which for MacNeice characterized the very soul of the city-dweller, and they are simply trains, harsh penetrators of country order and peace, far from the soothing rumble of his childhood. 'The peasant shambles on his boots like hooves / Without thinking at all or wanting to run in grooves.' From the 1930s onwards, MacNeice was to inveigh against any agents of mass salvation, anything seeking to undermine the strength of individuality, to blur uniqueness. In 'Turf-stacks' he deliberately trivializes his own preoccupations ('For we are obsolete who like the lesser things/ Who play in corners with looking-glasses and beads'), forestalling criticism by admitting a penchant for things shining, multi-coloured, narcissistic, confessing the insidious attraction of intellectual theorizing. Still MacNeice identifies his outlook with the phenomenon of natural destructiveness in a powerful closing simile, thus managing to ally himself with the peasant against the artificial life, destroyers before they are destroyed.

The question of MacNeice's relation to the South, or to Ireland as a whole, is puzzled out in many of the poems he wrote in the 1930s. Love and disillusionment co-existed, Dublin attracted him. Late in his life, MacNeice said that he had always found it 'a home away from home', while acknowledging that he had liked the city more than it had cared for him: 'Let him go back and labour / For Faber and Faber.'[16] The journey in 'Train to Dublin' (1934) is a journey of acceptance, a movement which perhaps parallels the physical distancing from the North. The poem concerns not only what we think about but also the way in which we think, and this MacNeice endeavours to convey with sensuous particularity, no longer by abstractions. Instead of division, he looks for an identity of the 'basic facts repatterned without pause' with the thoughts about them, an abandonment to perception. The danger for MacNeice was the fluency of his word-association, an alert mind indulgent to the pleasure of uncovering similarities, or simply seeing where assonance and rhyme could take a line of thought. In this poem though, revision curbs digression. Dublin and Ireland provide 'some surface to clutch', not in themselves important in the draft version of the poem, but treated with affectionate specificity in the final text.

'I give you the incidental things which pass / Outward through space exactly as each was': this might be taken as an abbreviation of MacNeice's current poetic manifesto. What immediately follows his declaration of intention is abstract, 'the disproportion between labour spent / And joy at random', seeming to veer away from the proposal, but the seventh and eighth stanzas continue to enumerate things passing. In re-writing the section, MacNeice eliminated earlier verbal tricks and internal rhyme; the slightly hysterical tone went, along with the original lame ending. He was becoming more critical. There are two large holograph notebooks in Mrs Hedli Mac-Neice's possession: of the forty-nine poems in the 1929-34 Notebook only eighteen were published; from its successor—ending in June 1936—fourteen out of twenty-seven. Rejected ideas, lines, images were used in poems that went into print, though not a great many; it may have seemed to MacNeice that, with material for poetry everywhere, there was no need to be thrifty. Most of the notebook work must have been copied out from earlier drafts, as there are few changes. Both 'Train to Dublin' and 'Ode', however, are substantially altered, sug-gesting that MacNeice found the direction of longish poems more difficult to control. From Birmingham he contributed poems to *New Verse*, with short accompanying letters that gave nothing away. 'This was the man who walked very, very much by himself—I mean he'd send you the poem. He wasn't going to talk about it, he wasn't going to discuss it. If you liked it well and good and that was that.'[17] So Geoffrey Grigson remembered, publishing 'Train to Dublin' in February 1935.

Apropos of that poem, F. O. Matthiessen remarked that MacNeice had evolved a 'neat craft of making the inner coherence of a poem depend on the subtle and precise inter-relationships of a series of things observed', the danger being that if any image asserts itself 'too vividly, the balance is upset and the whole effect falls into obtrusive fragments'.[18] Despite the avowed intention of 'Train to Dublin', the more successful effort is 'Valediction', where the objects' interrelationship is felt to be integral, exposed rather than imposed by the poet. Sustained in its dismay and anger, it was written earlier in the same year and at first entitled 'Eclogue on Ireland' (1929-34 Notebook). 'Valediction' is more appropriate to its intention and tone as there is no real discussion, not even MacNeice against himself. His position is clear from the beginning and there is no attempt at persuasion. This is the same tone that informs his references to Ireland in *Autumn Journal*: 'she gives her children neither sense nor money / Who slouch around the world with a gesture and a brogue / And a faggot of useless memories' (Canto XVI). 'Valediction' is fiercely resolved to resist the seductions that MacNeice cannot help enumerating.

The poem builds slowly to its climax. The opening is oblique, an odd sidling into the subject, with its repetitive first phrase and details that slowly coalesce. Whose 'verdure', what is being described as 'cant and randy', the subject of 'died ... sniped ... taken': none of this is exactly clear, perhaps only a sense of wetness and dumb brutality emerges. MacNeice turns from this to the world an outsider might encounter, Sackville Street and the statues of patriots, a history he treats more gently—in the simile 'old rings hollow-eyed without their stones'—than the present in Belfast. Ships' sirens recur, alongside 'minute sodden haycocks', the adjectives ruining any potential for fertility or gaiety. After he has mentioned both cities, it is as though MacNeice draws breath in the shorter lines to fuel his indignation—'I would say to you, Look'— which escapes possible petulance in the long, all but monosyllabic line:

> I would say, This is what you have given me
> Indifference and sentimentality
> A metallic giggle, a fumbling hand,
> A heart that leaps to a fife band:
> Set these against your water-shafted air
> Of amethyst and moonstone, the horses' feet like
>   bells of hair
> Shambling beneath the orange cart, the beer-brown
>   spring
> Guzzling between the heather, the green gush of
>   Irish spring.
> Cursèd be he that curses his mother. I cannot be
> Anyone else than what this land engendered me:

The precision of the passage is admirable: the quick shifts of tone, the balance of images. From personal traits, to generalized emotion, to landscape in romantic hues—the naming of stones which guarantees magic for MacNeice, but which he counters here with the stoutness of the spring, even slipping in the orange and the green—the movement of expansion is curtailed lest sentimentality take over, and the transitional tinge of melodrama is curbed by factual statement. 'Valediction' is scattered with this kind of checked emphasis, as though MacNeice is tacking slightly until he can trust himself to go directly ahead, and it gives a necessary tension to the structure, pulling against the regularity of the couplets.

MacNeice seems to insist that all the visitor sees is sham Irish charm, the facet that struck him as a child in Dublin—'what I chiefly noticed was a shopwindow with little souvenirs of bogoak and Connemara marble' ('Under the Sugar Loaf')—and the things with which the Irish charm themselves, the litany of heroic names. He sees the whole nation trapped by its past and its landscape 'in drug-dull fatalism'. Although he cannot 'deny my past to which my self is wed', he can attempt, in taut lines, to immunize himself, preserve himself in detachment. Some Irish critics have seen this willed separation as detrimental to his poetry, but MacNeice sensed that remaining in the country, where he would still be something of a foreigner by his upbringing and education, would involve him in a constant battle of definition: '... I must in course discuss / What we mean to Ireland or Ireland to us; / ... I have to gesture, / Take part in, or renounce each imposture'. From the line 'I will exorcise my blood', onwards, MacNeice is very sure of his direction: genuine loveliness is admitted and left behind in his decisive progress. His lyricism over the land was echoed later in prose:

An Irish landscape is capable of pantomimic transformation scenes; one moment it will be desolate, dead, unrelieved monotone, the next it will be an indescribably shifting pattern of prismatic light. ... I do not think it fanciful to maintain ... that there is something palpably in common between the subtle colour and movement of [Yeats's] verse and that western landscape which is at the same time delicate and strong. (*Yeats*, p. 50)

So in 'Valediction' MacNeice succeeded in matching his verse to the alacrity of light, the bleakness of factory files, and Ulster farms. He communicates a pastoral vision of Ireland in his list of animals, from peasants' hens to landowners' 'hunters beautifully bred', but the final line holds the country's terrors: 'Your drums and your dolled-up Virgins and your ignorant dead.' Protestant and Catholic, divided amongst themselves or against each other, responding only to violence, generating bitterness: this is the heritage he felt compelled to resign, exorcizing it through poetry.

Nevertheless, 'Farewell, my country, and in perpetuum' was premature. 'The South as a land of escape' continued to appear in the poems and, more hauntingly, 'the North of Ireland as prison'. Writing of the citizens of Belfast in *Zoo*, MacNeice temporarily settled his quarrel in prose: 'Who was I to condemn them? I was insulated with comfort and private memories. ... I had always dramatised them into the Enemy. They were not really grandiose monsters'. He allowed that 'even if I had adequate grounds for hating them, I still ought to make sure that I am not hating them mainly because I identify them with the nightmares of my childhood'. The year after 'Valediction' this sense of nightmare was articulated in 'Intimations of Mortality', which has no overt connection with Ireland, except that we know it was the warnings of a 'well-meaning but barbarous mother's help from County Armagh' which inspired at least part of the night-fear.[19]

Whereas in *Blind Fireworks* MacNeice had subscribed to a Sitwellian view of childhood ('... life seemed less a stranger, then,/ Than ever after in this cold existence', 'Colonel Fantock'), in which nightmares came lapped in gorgeous images, or draped in the pathetic fallacy, in *Poems* the same experience is transmitted in stark terms. Although he titled earlier poems 'Child's Terror' and 'Child's Unhappiness', and in them dwelt on time passing, death, and the problem of identity, their sensuous images, repetition, and lulling rhythms rob them of the real terror 'Intimations' conveys. The poems have in common changing perspectives, but in 1935 MacNeice was more adept in his control. 'Child's Unhappiness' escapes into lines purely decorative, as:

> Draw the velvet from his head
> Over that ominous regal bed,
> Reveal Apollo in sleep as fair
> As when Daphne half enjoyed despair.

Such elegance entirely removes it from the sphere of the child's supposed search for himself, or proof of his identity. The widening of the search, from the shelf on which the child feels he has been placed, to plumbing 'the veiled precipitate west'; the changing seasons, 'A shroud of yellow lace, a shroud of snow' ('Child's Terror'): these were no doubt intended to emphasize both the child's ease of identification with natural objects, and his feeling of insignificance in their shadow. Much more effective is the domesticity of the opening line of 'Intimations': 'The shadows of the banisters march march', the dissociation from the first person so that the poem can be inside the boy's mind and observing it. From the contentment darkness brings to the lovers, lingering in concealment, the stanza expands to include the normally soothing sea-sound, that here becomes insidious, as though its stealth partly causes wakefulness: 'On the beach the waves creep,/ The little boy cannot go to sleep.' It has a nursery-rhyme simplicity of diction, God and the Devil enter the poem on the same matter-of-fact footing as the sea and the banisters. At the end of the third stanza, the appearance of a lamp restores order, and the first metaphor, accompanying it, has a reassuring solidity, 'Time on horseback under a Roman arch', halted in its march. The fear of clocks ticking out of silence, and of falling, comes in a nervous rush, plainly. In 'Child's Terror' ('I fell in a nightmare down suddenly / Into a hole without a bottom') the slight awkwardness of the phrasing attests to the pressure of this memory on MacNeice, which he refines in 'Intimations', re-enacting the sensation in the line-break; 'The tick of his pulse in the pillow, the sick / Vertigo of falling in a fanged pit': regularity produced by alliteration, internal rhyme, and then the drop to 'vertigo', looping to the finality of 'pit'.

'Child's Terror' ends in desperation, but is swaddled in a self-conscious literary language—'Turn a light on my snowy counterpane, ... /And the pampas grass will raise plume aloft again—'—which becomes a pose in 'Child's Unhappiness': 'I faint as memoried distress / In the mouth melts to forgetfulness'.[20] The real terror emerges in 'Intimations' by means of a telescopic enlargement that has no end: 'The night watchman with crossed thumbs / Grows an idol. The Kingdom comes...'. The prayer a child might say to ward off evil takes on infinitely sinister meaning.

The last pre-war exploration of childhood and Ireland occurs in *The Earth Compels* (1938). 'Carrickfergus' is direct autobiography and signals that taut style of the volume as a whole. The brisk movement of the verse matches its observations of external factors, there is nothing introspective or speculative. Objects are catalogued with adult detachment, yet they possess that solidity they have for a child, who sees them in juxtaposition without distinguishing them in terms of value: the terrier's yapping and the soldiers' singing make an equal impact on the consciousness. This picture of Carrickfergus is dominated by the War, an incomprehensible event, MacNeice recalled, because 'all foreigners were foreigners to me and at first I could not distinguish between the English and the Germans'.[21] It was also the period of his mother's departure and death (1914), and his own dispatch to Sherborne (1917). None of the emotional turmoil is recorded. Perhaps MacNeice did not remember, as Lady Nicholson vividly did, the lines of weeping women coming to the rectory for comfort in July 1916. ('First, the Ulster Division at the Somme / Going over the top with "Fuck the Pope!"')[22] Except for an identifying sentence in the fifth stanza, 'Carrickfergus' is a public poem, while it escapes the charge of journalism sometimes levelled against MacNeice.

The almost jaunty rhythm of its quatrains conveys none of the brooding, subdued fury of 'Belfast'; no item is dwelt upon, no scene intensified by adjectives in the manner of the earlier poem's 'melancholy lough / Against the lurid sky over the stained water'. The vocabulary, too, is spare, so that the one note of flamboyance has resonance: 'Under the peacock aura of a drowning moon'.

> I was the rector's son, born to the anglican order,
>   Banned for ever from the candles of the Irish poor;
> The Chichesters knelt in marble at the end of a transept
>   With ruffs about their necks, their portion sure.

It is an economical notation of alienation: the candles carry a hint of liveliness and warmth as well as poverty, set against the arrogance of the Elizabethan monument in his father's church, confident of gaining heaven, and secure in their earthly glory founded on their exploitation of precisely the Irish poor. Following 'sure' with 'The war came' in the next stanza, and the springing up of a military camp, at least partially undercuts any sense of order.

There is perhaps no other poem that touches on World War I from this perspective. The difference war makes to the appearance of familiar, civilian territory is the only way it might be expected to impinge on a child. Graves, Blunden, and Sassoon all register in memoirs their notion that the War would never end, and in 'Carrickfergus' this conviction is domesticated by MacNeice:

> I thought that the war would last for ever and sugar
> Be always rationed and that never again

> Would the weekly papers not have photos of sandbags
> And my governess not make bandages from moss
> And people not have maps above the fireplace
> With flags on pins moving across and across—

The great accumulation of heroic myth, in the shadow of which MacNeice's generation grew up, is entirely excluded from the poem. The isolation he experiences is both that of a Protestant rector's son, and that common to children sent away to school, whose world become completely separate from that of their family and town: 'the world of parents / Contracted into a puppet world of sons'. With the transition from smoky Carrickfergus to Dorset the sense of division is confirmed; henceforth the poems about Ireland and childhood betray a suspicion that paradise had been on the margins of both, irrecoverable by art.

For a while, despite the impression given in later essays, MacNeice had not quite belonged to Birmingham either. His wife found the city unalluring and created an island for their marriage, a home as multicoloured as a gipsy caravan, where poetry was not taken seriously. For MacNeice it may have been a return to the remembered domestic warmth of his earliest years. He could manage optimism about the human capacity to make what it will of time, condemning:

> The pathetic fallacy of the passing hours
> When it is we who pass them—hours of stone,
> Long rows of granite sphinxes looking on.

> It is we who pass them, we the circus masters
> Who make the mayflies dance, the lapwings lift
>   their crests,

Yet the reassertion indicates a lack of conviction, and 'Mayfly' ends on a dramatic capitulation to time: 'But when this summer is over let us die together,/ I want always to be near your breasts'. This is the first entrance of a loved person into the poems, which are on the whole firmly self-centred.

His new preoccupations, however, were not proof against the movement of the year, which from this time terrified him. 'The buoyant months are May and June. Once they are over, I feel defeated.'[23] MacNeice gave poetic expression to this feeling in 'August', in which he is concerned, obliquely, with the inability of art as well as of people to follow 'the living curve which is breathlessly the same'. Frames and limits have a tendency to petrify experience, yet there is a grace in their artifice, and MacNeice himself puts his thoughts into end-stopped quatrains that secure each image. The ease with which he moves, inside one stanza, from Poussin to lawn-mowers shows his growing ability to use the props of contemporary life without self-consciousness, as in the camera-image of the striking opening line: 'The shutter of time darkening ceaselessly'. The gathering formality of the verse works to a conclusion that reads like a classical translation, fit for the sundial or garden-statue's plinth:

> But all this is a dilettante's lie,
> Time's face is not stone nor still his wings;
> Our mind, being dead, wishes to have time die
> For we, being ghosts, cannot catch hold of things.

It is as though, when he chose to describe so precisely the world in which he moved and fix it in the poems, MacNeice knew the effort to be inadequate from the outset. This gives the edge of melancholy or sombreness that rescues the poems from triviality. For all that he proclaimed in 'Wolves' that he did not 'want / To be always stressing either its flux or its permanence', MacNeice's poems swing between the two, notably in 'Sunday Morning'.

The poem begins by describing 'a weekly moment of choice which Louis and Mary shared with a thousand other young couples, and laments its passing (Louis loved fast cars)'.[24] While the surburban Sunday is rendered in terms of its sounds, without any strain the dimension beyond space and time is also brought into play. The philosophical point springs from a simple, common experience: Monday's pressure is just discernible, how then to make the most of 'free' time? By saying that the morning is 'Fate's great bazaar'—a typical MacNeice phrase—he removes some of this sense of freedom, and the self-generated limitations emerge. The nimble scales 'may grow to music' but the most one can realistically hope for is 'to drive beyond Hindhead' at a speed that removes one from the working week. Perhaps it restores that carelessness, living in the 'Now' that existed before work and responsibilities had to be acknowledged; 'the windy past' alive with movement. MacNeice's own past would not let him ignore the counterpoint provided by the church bells, which had for him 'a sinister association', though as he remarked: 'I have rationalised or twisted my original association which would have suggested rather "escape from *Sunday* time", i.e. from that stony, joyless anti-time of the church (my upbringing was puritanical) which had seemed to preclude music and movement and the growth of anything but stalactites and stalagmites.'[25]

The ghost of sonnet form is summoned by the metaphor MacNeice finds for the Sunday effort to outpace the week; the poem has the traditional fourteen lines, but the thought breaks between the tenth and eleventh lines rather than after the octave, and the whole is written in couplets. MacNeice's technical assurance is particularly noticeable in the closing quatrain, where thought is carried across the line-endings to imitate the inexorability of the bells:

> But listen, up the road, something gulps, the church
>   spire
> Opens its eight bells out, skulls' mouths which will
>   not tire
> To tell how there is no music or movement which
>   secures
> Escape from the weekday time. Which deadens
>   and endures.

The MacNeices' close, dependent relationship, detached from its Birmingham context, underwent a change with the birth of their son Daniel in May 1934. In the 1929-34 Notebook

MacNeice copied out a poem about the child's ancestry, a vivid evocation of the peasant origins he liked to claim—'Their hair stands up like bog-grass & their clothes / Smell of peat'—and of the sensual, troubled, cosmopolitan background of his Jewish wife: 'They have been merchants & wise men whose hands / Can draw out pain and test the pile of silks'. At some stage he must have felt the poem worthy of inclusion in a projected volume, as it was not deleted nor marked 'omit' as were many in the notebook. In the end the two lines of patient ghosts, ignoring each other and waiting for 'a child of you & me to come down this street / & run the gauntlet of such ancestors', may have seemed too private an image to expose.

He did compose and publish a lengthy poem for his son, requesting a return to 'homeliness'. Certainly the opening lines of 'Ode' are homely enough: 'To-night is so coarse with chocolate / The wind blowing from Bournville / That I hanker after the Atlantic'. The poem turns out to be less for Daniel than a meditation to help the poet arrange things in his own mind. Although the references are accessible without biographical knowledge, with it they become less random. In the first stanza the connection between MacNeice's hankering for the Atlantic and the longing of film fans seems less forced when we consider what the Irish coast meant to him, and also the degree to which he felt alien to the routine of Birmingham:

When the wind blew from the south the air would thicken with chocolate; we were only a mile from the Cadbury Works. ... The girls in their white aprons each with her own little monotony, ... [bonbons] are shot round the world to people's best girls and mothers and the frilly paper is trampled underfoot in cinemas and railway trains and stadiums and every day is somebody's birthday. (*Strings*, p. 132)

This distaste for whatever is produced *en masse* is extended to anything that might be construed as limitless. 'Ode' is a plea for the recognition of particularity and yet it is conducted in oddly general terms: 'I want a sufficient sample, the exact and framed/Balance of definite masses, the islanded hour.' Sample, balance, and distinction are the poem's methods.

The ostensible occasion for the 'Ode' is not immediately apparent; once it becomes so, Yeats's 'A Prayer for My Daughter' is brought to mind, with its 'haystack and roof-levelling wind, / Bred on the Atlantic'. Neither man wishes intellectual gifts for his child. MacNeice asks that he have 'five good senses / The feeling for symmetry', and then in quasi-Yeatsian terms that the boy escape wearing a hollow mask, able to be, as Yeats has it, 'Rooted in one dear perpetual place'.

By the eleventh stanza, he abandons the attempt to make this delineation of the golden mean ('Which contains the seasonal extreme') directly relevant to his son's future. Mac-Neice's central dilemma emerges: how to make the 'blessedness of fact' immediate and lasting, how to maintain the balancing act without being false to emotion and experience. He mimes in the personal context an act of revolutionary decisiveness, neither regretful nor vacillating:

> We must cut the throat of the hour
> That it may not haunt us because our sentiments
> Continued its existence to pollute
> Its essence; bottled time turns sour upon the sill.

Typically, MacNeice concludes an imperious announcement with an image from daily life, tempering the impossibly dramatic.

This life, however, includes the present threat. Samuel Hynes sees 'Ode' as representative of its disordered decade in the way it is 'invaded by public elements—mob mania, newspapers, a bombing plane, Europe—which are all threats to a fulfilled private life for his infant son'; for the father, too. [26] There is, Hynes continues, 'a sense of violation of intimate private occasions', bodied in passages such as this, in the eighteenth stanza:

> But this identical sound the then epitome
> Of summer's athletic ease and the smell of cut grass
> Will sometime be our augury of war
> When these tiny flies like nibs will calmly draw our
>   death
> A dipping gradient on the graph of Europe

MacNeice presumably liked the image, as he used it in *Modern Poetry* to exemplify 'the blend of cerebral and sensuous ... almost a metaphysical image, but the picture of the moving aeroplanes is intended to persist' (p. 112). As he had long since broadened his perspective beyond the occasion of birth, the entrance of the planes does not take its force from a contrast with intimacy. If anything violates the predominantly meditative tone of the poem, it is the next stanza, where MacNeice moves by associational logic to the town-dweller, suffering and alienated from his environment, who like a rabbit 'Hangs by the heels gut-open against the fog / Between two spires that are not conscious of him'.

When he comes to drawing conclusions they are not especially for his son's benefit, reverting to the subject of his own temptations.

> But as others, forgetting the others,
>   Run after the nostrums
> Of science art and religion
>   So would I mystic and maudlin
> Dream of the both real and ideal
>   Breakers of ocean.
> I must put away this drug.

The desire to escape into an unreal world, whether dignified by mysticism or not, has to be rejected, though it occurs again and again in MacNeice's poems. 'Breakers of ocean' takes us back to the beginning of 'Ode', and there too they were seductive, despite his nostalgia's being labelled 'frivolous'. The pressure the birth exerts on the poet's life is resisted in so far as it might lead to a false construction, however he admits to a kind of Romantic yearning for an existence 'innocent and integral', where the real and ideal merge. The poem ends in imperfect peace: the waves threaten absolute serenity.

MacNeice admits in the poem that he 'cannot draw up any code / There are too many qualifications'. It was his first important attempt at working out a philosophical position in poetry; it reveals him as given neither to steady introspection nor to tough intellectual reasoning, but principally to delight in the physical world and a lauding of instinct, of emotional response. At Oxford he had felt the attraction of transcendentalism, yet the contradictions in his environment were not sufficiently accounted for by any variation on a doctrine of Forms. 'Ode' demonstrates the pull of universalizing; yet, as E. R. Dodds—a good friend and Professor of Greek at Birmingham —suggests, MacNeice wrote best when his poems were rooted in immediate personal experience.

Such a one is 'Snow', conceived on a winter's evening at the Dodds's house. 'Out of doors it was snowing, but in the study window Bet had placed a big bowl of roses from our heated greenhouse, ''soundlessly collateral and incompatible'', while we sat round the fire eating tangerines. The scene was no invented symbol ...' (*Missing Persons*, p. 117). The poem appears in the 1934-6 Notebook, with two alterations in the second stanza. 'Indomitably plural' is replaced by 'incorrigibly', the earlier choice being fractionally less flexible. The other change is 'various' for 'different', alliteration not providing quite the sense of expansiveness his euphoria demands. In a letter to John Hilton in 1930, MacNeice had called for 'lots of lovely particulars; I suggest keeping generalisations out of it ...', but in 'Snow' the general statement flowers from specific details, leaves a space for mystery without depriving snow, fire, roses, and tangerines of their richness.

Although apparently content in that poem with both the evidence of his senses and what he made of it, in others there is a distrust of words, tempering the astonished delight which is the well-spring of 'Snow'.

> So we whose senses give us things misfelt and misheard
> Turn also, for our adjustment, to the pretentious word
> Which stabilises the light on the sun-fondled trees
> And, by photographing our ghosts, claims to put
>   us at our ease;   ('Nature Morte')

By using the camera metaphor, MacNeice implies that the act of selection made by the artist necessarily involves a degree of distortion, while the illusion is of stability and substance. Turning from people to objects, from photography to painting, the medium becomes transparent:

>   even a still life is alive
> And in your Chardin the appalling unrest of the soul
> Exudes from the dried fish and the brown jug and
>   the bowl.

Nevertheless, having to rely on 'the pretentious word', MacNeice endeavoured to portray a world of terrifying flux: insouciant as his poems often appear, his personal, fearful obsession is with time.

II. THE THIRTIES: PUBLIC PLACES

MacNeice's sense of transience and profound unrest, whose private sources have been indicated, was fostered by the anxieties of the period, the suspicion of existing in parenthesis. When Auden and Day Lewis edited *Oxford Poetry* in 1927, they contributed a preface anticipating one of the most pressing literary problems of the next decade: 'All genuine poetry is in a sense the formation of private spheres out of public chaos...'.[1] The relation of the one to the other troubled MacNeice, until he temporarily found a poetic solution in the dexterous counterpoint of *Autumn Journal*.

At a time of manifestos, groups, analysis, MacNeice like others of his generation issued statements about art with apparent facility. His may be distinguished, however, by a wry tone, an inability to subscribe to even Auden's seductive moral imperatives. Generalizations prefaced shrewd attention to particulars, as in his contribution to Grigson's symposium, *The Arts To-day*:

The best poets of to-day belong to, and write for, cliques. The cliques, lately, have not been purely literary; they identify themselves with economic, political or philosophical movements. This identification is more fruitful when it is voluntary; ... The best English poets have been those most successfully determined by their context. ... The English context is now more congenial to poets than it has been for a long time. (pp. 30-1)

The slightly waspish remark about the nature of a writer's identification marks the passage as MacNeice's: the underlining of the poets' social context perhaps reveals the stamp of the decade. Aware of the danger contemporary poetry ran, of being 'judged by its party colours', he still welcomed the 'intoxication with a creed' as being 'a good antidote to defeatist individualism' of the kind found in Prufrock and Mauberley.[2] He resisted being carried away himself, just as he eschewed some features he thought notable in the poetry of his contemporaries: ' ... the topical, the gnomic and the heroic; these poets make myths of themselves and of each other. ... Comradeship is the communist substitute for bourgeois romance; in its extreme form ... it leads to an idealisation of homosexuality.'[3] MacNeice was outside the clique in his almost aggressive heterosexuality, and it was not until the 1950s that he constructed his own poetic myths of friendship. The 'gnomic' is particularly Auden's contribution: mysterious landscapes and journeys; nameless figures receiving hermetic instructions; both protagonists and readers being urged to moral judgement, moments of choice. Topicality was their common factor: there was 'material for poetry everywhere'.[4]

MacNeice enlarged on these themes in 'Subject in Modern Poetry', adopting the distinction Auden had made concerning the moral function of art. Auden had declared, in his essay for Grigson's survey, that 'there must always be two kinds of art, escape-art, for man needs escape as he needs food and deep sleep, and parable-art, that art which shall teach man to unlearn hatred and learn love ...'.[5] Conceding that Auden's poetry embraces both categories, MacNeice assigns Eliot and Yeats to escape, Auden and Spender to parable, a concept he was to find especially useful in discussing poetry in the 1960s. What gives life to contemporary poetry, provides its vital literary context is, he suggests, a combination of 'the pity of Owen, the Whitmanesque lust for life of Lawrence, and the dogmas of Lenin'.[6] This prefigures MacNeice's plea for 'impure poetry'; Auden and Spender are esteemed for their 'great gift of compromise'. The world is of value and interest, contemporary life should be written about—at least indirectly—and because they are part of the poets' environment,

pylons and gasometers are not merely *décor*. The modern poet is very conscious that he is writing in and of an industrial epoch and that what expresses itself visibly in pylons and gasometers is the same force that causes the discontent and discomfort of the modern individual, the class-warfare of modern society, and wars between nations in the modern world.[7]

This is the most politicized statement about poetry that Mac-Neice ever made. It probably amused him to have it appear under the staid auspices of the English Association, but it was not just a nod in the correct, Marxist direction. The sentence may be seen as both a justification and a way out of a dilemma; a strategy is implied. In writing about urban and industrial surroundings, the poet indicates an awareness of the forces behind them without having to spell out his lesson. A poet disbelieving in political progress may thus acknowledge the existence of wounds he sees no prospect of being healed.

'Birmingham' is almost surrealist at times in MacNeice's effort to convey the way material objects impinge upon and govern urban lives: 'Cubical scent-bottles artificial legs arctic foxes and electric mops'. (Larkin perhaps owes something to the poem in 'Here', *The Whitsun Weddings*.) Objects are given human characteristics—'the queue of fidgety machines', 'half-timbered houses with lips pressed / So tightly'—and people become indistinguishable among the streets they walk:

> The lunch hour: the shops empty, shopgirls' faces relax
> Diaphanous as green glass, empty as old almanacs
> As incoherent with ticketed gewgaws tiered behind their heads
> As the Burne-Jones windows in St Philip's broken by crawling leads;

Debasement spreads. Emotion in this setting is mechanical too, reserved for a weekend spree, 'the heart's fun-fair'. It is difficult to pin down the attitude towards the city and its inhabitants that this poem betrays. There is certainly contempt for suburbia, 'In these houses men as in a dream pursue the Platonic Forms / With wireless and cairn terriers ...', a contempt for those aspiring to middle-class values, 'climbing tentatively upward on jerry-built beauty and sweated labour'. The finale begins extravagantly, conjuring traffic against a sunset sky, with MacNeice taking pleasure in finding the exact shades for the lights—'crème-de-menthe or bull's blood'— and revelling in the obedience of the machine, its 'engine gently breathing'. Then colour drains from the lines as the factory chimneys appear, which 'on sullen sentry will all night wait / To call, in the harsh morning, sleep-stupid faces through the daily gate'. The tone is no longer dismissive, rather it resentfully accepts stolid fact, unalterable by any words.

In 1934 MacNeice was proposing at least five books for publication over the next year. The most likely of these was a collection of poems that T. S. Eliot had provisionally approved, though requiring that they be rearranged: 'That was one for

me as I had taken great trouble arranging them in their present
order. However, I am going to scrap some more and see what
I can do. ... Also I shall have time to include one or two eclogues. These I find have great possibilities. There is going
to be one all about my education.'[8] According to MacNeice in
The Strings Are False, he discovered the potential of this form at
Christmas in 1933. As his wife submerged herself in preparations for their first child, he looked outwards and discovered
his contemporaries 'swallowing Marx with the same naïve
enthusiasm that made Shelley swallow Rousseau'. Unable to
sink his ego that way, he still found himself entirely sympathetic
to 'their hatred of the *status quo*'. The way he found to express
an urge to destruction was the deliberate composition of 'An
Eclogue for Christmas': 'I wrote it with a kind of cold-blooded
passion and when it was done it surprised me. Was I really as
concerned as all that with the Decline of the West? Did I really
feel so desperate? Apparently I did. Part of me must have been
feeling like that for years.'[9] It was published in *New Verse* (April
1934); 'Valediction: an eclogue' appeared in *Life and Letters*
(April/September 1934), and when *Poems* was published by
Faber and Faber in 1935, these two opened the collection,
followed by 'Eclogue by a Five-barred Gate'.

MacNeice had experimented with dialogue before, in 'A
Conventional Serenade' (*Blind Fireworks*). Amyas, the protagonist, addresses a Rustick, himself, and an Owl, but the
dominant mode is Marvell out of Eliot and the voices are not
differentiated. The eclogues in *Poems*, however, have a genuinely dialectical structure. MacNeice's detachment, irony,
divided spirit, found its apt poetic medium in these, as in
Autumn Journal. The eclogues allowed debate without requiring
a resolution, while their statement and counter-statement
helped improve the construction of his poetry. He was not
always able to impose a clarifying order on his impressions,
could just slide from one to the next. Although MacNeice
maintained in *Modern Poetry* that it was sometimes only in the
act of writing that the poet became sure of what he wanted to
say—'he works up to his meaning by a dialectic of purification'
—in practice he sometimes appeared insufficiently rigorous
in his consideration of the finished poem. The eclogues escape
such criticism.

It is not simply the static dialogue form, nor even the convention of shepherds, that MacNeice takes from the eclogue tradition. He needed to look back no further than Yeats for a master in the former, as in the volumes he would have recently read, *Words for Music Perhaps* and *The Winding Stair*. Eclogues are associated with that pastoral genre to which, W. W. Greg contends, 'a sense of the contrast between town and country was essential'. He maintains that this contrast animates various kinds of pastoral: 'the ideal where it breeds desire for a return to simplicity, [of] the realistic where the humour of it touches the imagination, and [of] the allegorical where it suggests satire on the corruption of an artificial civilization'.[10] Three out of MacNeice's four eclogues are clearly in the ideal/allegorical tradition, where some degree of degeneracy is presumed: 'Valediction', which dropped its subtitle in *Poems*, nevertheless contains criticism of a predominantly rural and unsophisticated society from an outsider's viewpoint; while 'Eclogue Between the Motherless' is patently a dialogue between analogues of the self, and has nothing to say about society.

MacNeice's account of the composition of 'An Eclogue for Christmas' seems to suggest that it was a 'given' poem, its definite shape taking the author by surprise. Some images surfaced from previous poems, however, such as the striking lines: 'I who was Harlequin in the childhood of the century, / Posed by Picasso beside an endless opaque sea,' a version of the opening of a deleted poem, 'For some time poets have been harlequins or playboys' (1929-34 Notebook). Perhaps this passage is the residue of MacNeice's reading of 'Prufrock', the speaker standing aside to assess what society has made of its victim. While Prufrock considers spiritual consequences, A sees the result in aesthetic terms and in autobiographical ones, if we identify 'A' with MacNeice.

In his last, intellectually heady year at Marlborough, with Anthony Blunt as mentor, MacNeice had discovered Modern Art and both of them, under the spell of Roger Fry and Clive Bell, believed 'without any qualification in Pure Form'.[11] Blunt, in his retrospective survey 'From Bloomsbury to Marxism', explicitly links the worship of abstraction with the prevailing social ignorance that was to continue throughout his undergraduate years at Cambridge and MacNeice's time at

Oxford: a period of 'complete unreality, ... we lived in this little self-contained world of art and literature, with no awareness of what was taking place in the outside world at all.' Or as MacNeice phrases it in the 'Eclogue', 'Without reference to this particular life'. When writing the poem, he must have been conscious of the change in Blunt's life, since 'quite suddenly, in the autumn term of 1933, Marxism hit Cambridge'. The artists praised in the 1920s were either demoted or approved on quite different grounds; the real danger was perceived to lie 'in Cubism, which began the final movement away from humanist painting and led towards abstraction, towards an art which had lost all contact, we thought, with the general public, with humanity at large ...'. MacNeice put his own rejection in A's mouth: 'They have made of me pure form, a symbol or a pastiche, / Stylised profile, anything but soul and flesh'. He elaborated the thought in a contribution to the Auden number of *New Verse*, after a misquotation from Marx: '"Other philosophies have described the world, our business is to change it." ... if we are not interested in changing it, there is really very little to describe. There is just an assortment of heterogeneous objects to make Pure Form out of.'[12]

It is doubtful that 'An Eclogue for Christmas' offers potential for change, the speakers appear to accept their doom with a kind of morbid relish. The countryman, B, notes that 'the moon's glare, / Goggling yokel-stubborn through the iron trees, / Jeers at the end of us, our bland ancestral ease;' an ease and landscape MacNeice is not quite so skilled at portraying as he is the 'beauty narcotic and deciduous' acknowledged by A, the city-dweller. Even this slight uncertainty might be accounted part of the pastoral tradition of the urban observer's distance from the rural setting he praises. In the end both speakers determine to indulge themselves in ways of life already established, finding refuge in living for the self. The dialogue form protects MacNeice from the accusation of endorsing a reactionary code: if he is identified with any statement in the poem, it is perhaps with B's closing lines, 'Let all these so ephemeral things / Be somehow permanent like the swallow's tangent wings'. This is the volume he chose to preface with the line from *Agamemnon* ('like a boy who chases a flying bird'); the poems are suffused with a sense of the necessity and futility of an effort to capture the transient. The image had a particular connection for MacNeice, recalling his penultimate summer term at Oxford, punting up the Isis with his fiancée: '... one evening at twilight a squadron of swallows swooped down over the water, their reflections were been and gone, a moment of annunciation. I felt very near to Mariette and it was a relief not to have to discuss if the descent of swallows was "significant".' (Strings, p. 122) After the natural austerity evoked by B, and the hedonism of A, the swallow lines lift the poem from nostalgia to real yearning, so that the reminder of the Incarnation that ends the poem is saved from being dismissive or sneering, hints at its mystery.

The 'Eclogue by a Five-barred Gate', openly playing with its form, is also a narrative and an allegory. It is a distant precursor of some of MacNeice's radio dialogues, a less subtle version of his turn to parable in the sixties. The narrative closes with the death of the two shepherds, who go through the gate on an echo from Lycidas. The vision was undoubtedly apocalyptic, in its odd form, and Apocalypse was a pervasive theme of the decade. Whereas the Christmas eclogue expresses it in the appropriate social context, here it is more subdued, but the conclusions are similar: the importance of words against inevitable endings.

Quite different in scope from the others is the 'Eclogue Between the Motherless'. There is no record of its composition, and it does not appear in the notebooks containing much of the material for Poems and The Earth Compels, the volume in which it was published. The 1934-6 Notebook contains a few poems on Mary MacNeice's departure (she abruptly left MacNeice and their son in December 1935), and the blue-covered notebook (Buffalo) with many of the poems for Letters from Iceland, has various deleted drafts on the same theme, so it may be dated 1936. Unlike the other eclogues, with their parodic or satiric elements, this is unrelievedly sombre and revolves around a personal dilemma. Although the speakers are identified as 'motherless', their discussion concerns their loverless state, and the connection is the more disturbing for its remaining unstated, hovering. Its form encourages a much less self-pitying presentation of loneliness than in some of the poems of this period. MacNeice can both warn—'One marries only /

Because one thinks one is lonely—and so one was / But wait till the lonely are two and no better'—and bleakly pursue: 'There I sat / Concocting a gambler's medicine; the afternoon was cool, / The ducks drew lines of white on the dull slate of the pool'. The poem is moving because of the personal experience of double desertion MacNeice brings to it, and the universal longing he taps: for love that is 'heaven come back from the nursery—swansdown kisses', or the search for the 'perfect stranger'. The resolution A finds, contracting marriage with a dying woman, gives the relationship its limit, importantly ensures that its end is no one's 'fault'. The eclogue shows MacNeice's delight in female vitality: 'The hard light of sun upon water in diamonds dancing / And the brute swagger of the sea;' a comparison made again in 'Leaving Barra', 'While you are alive beyond question / Like the dazzle on the sea, my darling'. And there is a grim combination of his childhood nightmares with the image of his unborn child's ancestry found in an unpublished poem (mentioned above, p. 18): 'Helpless at the feet of faceless family idols / Walking the tightrope over the tiger pit, / Running the gauntlet of inherited fears'.

A more public realm of inheritance is explored in the last of the eclogues, also written in 1936 and published as part of the *Letters from Iceland* in 1937. MacNeice had been to Spain with Blunt for the Easter of 1936, undertaking the Icelandic commission with Auden in August and September. They were his first trips outside the British Isles since his marriage, a mixture of diversion—'I have come north, gaily running away / From the grinding gears, ... / The ambushes of sex, ...'—and quest: 'the crude / Embryo rummages every latitude / Looking for itself, its nature, its final pattern' ('Letter to Graham and Anna'). The number of travel books written in the 1930s is one sign of the English intelligentsia's awareness that wherever things were happening, it was not at home; the sense of diminishment was strong. MacNeice's instinct, however, was not to head for the centres of artistic, intellectual, or political innovation. In his autobiography he emphasized that the trip to Spain had no political implications: 'Our new revelation was the painting of Zurbaran. ...a lyrical intense placidity; a haunting matter-of-factness' (*Strings*, p. 159). Discussions with Blunt about the future of Communism became visions of an artistic revolution, a paean to the new medium: 'concrete is vital'. Instead he retreated, to Iceland and later to the Hebrides, looking at communities where traditional patterns of living, though doomed, might hold.

Hynes concludes, unsurprisingly, that the journey to Iceland was interesting to the poets as an opportunity to meditate on themselves rather than their ostensible subject. The book they produced, 'though it appears to record a temporary escape from Europe and the present, is really about the generation's inescapable involvement in its time, and in contemporary European disasters ...' (p. 289). Auden's attachment to Anglo-Saxon and Norse/Teutonic literature is well known, that they attracted MacNeice is less obvious. Like Auden, he would have responded to its dwelling on the theme of exile, on homes longed for and destroyed. Certainly he ranked Dasent's translation of *Burnt Njal* with his 'sacred books' at Marlborough, and he adapted Icelandic sagas for radio in 1947: *The Death of Gunnar, The Burning of Njal,* and *Grettir the Strong.*

It is Grettir who makes a ghostly appearance in the 'Eclogue from Iceland'. He is a less sympathetic hero than Njal, but may have appealed to MacNeice in this context because the saga compares him to Audun of Audunarstad. Auden himself is sketched in the speaker Craven, MacNeice in Ryan, in the dialogue with Grettir. The theme of the poem is appropriate both to the eclogue, in its comparison of a sophisticated society with a simpler past, and to the saga, whose authors tended to look back from an age of deceit and corruption to a time of integrity and honour. Like them, MacNeice is not interested in idealizing the past, yet through Grettir he conveys the strangeness, superhuman action, and magnitude of scale of Icelandic life, which the nineteenth-century translators such as Dasent and William Morris tried to communicate. MacNeice obviously knew the first, and possibly the second, of Morris's sonnets on Grettir; his own eclogue thus links him with the late Victorian passion for the Nordic past. As he flippantly expresses it in 'Letter to Graham and Anna':

> I will set forth
> The obscure but powerful ethics of Going North.
> Morris did it before, dropping the frills and fuss,
> Harps and arbours, Tristram and Theseus,
> For a land of rocks and sagas.

Prefaces to the *Collected Poems* do not indicate that the 'Eclogue from Iceland' differs from the version published in *Letters from Iceland*. The extant draft of the poem is of the first and longer version, marked 'for New Writing', the first issue of which had appeared in the spring of 1936. MacNeice altered it by excising most of the initial conversation before Grettir's appearance. Reference will be made to three stages of the text: A being the Buffalo draft (in the blue-covered notebook), B as it appears in *Letters*, C its form in the *Collected Poems*. A and B make what Craven and Ryan leave behind them more explicit and personal. They are presented as two men who at home lead a regular, bourgeois life—'kowtowing to boss or wife' (B; 'wage or wife': A)—but who, in wanting to 'stay here a week like a placid brute' (A and B), express a desire to escape from external pressure towards conformity. Moreover, they wish to be delivered from particular nightmares, and here perhaps the poets' 'real' personalities are hinted at, with Craven's 'Never dream of the empty church' and Ryan's *déjà vu* scene of abandonment: 'Nor of waiting in the familiar porch / With the broken bellpull, but the name / Above the door is not the same'. Ryan's lines in the draft, '& beside this cold and cutting stream / We should sleep and never dream' become in B more murmurous, lulling: 'And beside this cold and silicate stream / To sleep in sheepskin, never dream'.

The entrance of Grettir in A and B is prefaced by Ryan's saying 'Who could it be? / Except the echo of you and me', giving Grettir a role as the projection of an interior running debate, not just a saga ghost. It was omitted with the other lines—thirty three in all—perhaps because MacNeice felt that too lengthy an approach to the meeting lessened its drama.

MacNeice constructs for Grettir speech both slightly archaic and colloquial, full of phrases that might be proverbial or quasi-formulaic. Grettir characterizes Craven as 'You with crowsfeet round your eyes', Ryan as 'you with the burglar's underlip':

> Too many people. My memory will go,
> Lose itself in the hordes of modern people.
> Memory is words; we remember what others
> Say and record of ourselves—stones with the runes. (C)

The statement is ambiguous: the memory of Grettir will 'lose itself in the hordes of subject modern peoples' (A), that is, the example of a man whom disaster kept witty and restless will be lost; and in time his own memory will go, becoming less secure with each encounter. Originally MacNeice wanted to make the point that:

memory

~~Subjective & objective~~ [————], ~~closer connected~~

~~Than is commonly thought, / here renders what others~~

Say & record of oneself—Stones with the runes. (A)

Gravestones runically carved mean that death freezes memory, but might be interpreted in the wider context of the stony landscape where the dialogue takes place, which tells its own story, and summons its ghost, serving as the grave of the sagas.

On the other hand, the alteration of Ryan's following speech, which in A reads:

diehard

My countrymen like [————] drayhorses

Bludgeoned with sectarian religion

Drag their own deaths behind them.

~~Snipers on the roof tops for~~

generalizes the comment and, in so doing, strengthens it. The same phasing out of emotive words, only more ruthlessly because he is less involved in the country, occurs in the reference to Spain given to Craven (although Auden did not visit the country until the Civil War had broken out). The draft begins: 'This Easter I was in Spain which now is burning', becomes cavalier: 'This Easter I was in Spain lucky to get my month', returns to the dramatic, '... before the bombs', and finally seizes on the factual: '... before the Civil War'. The line 'Why shd I ~~bother~~ trouble who was only looking for dope' has a journalistic turn that matches the earlier admission, 'It was all copy', but it prompted him to change the self-description to 'addict to petty drugs', which appears in B and C as 'addict to oblivion' (without the melodrama of A's further qualification, 'the gloved exile'). As it stands, the phrase is reminiscent of 'Ode': 'I must put away this drug.' The tug of nothingness, repellent and seductive, reappears throughout the poetry.

While his manner of speaking is successful in the main, Grettir is made to take risks with language as his last way of living on the edge. 'I was the doomed tough' is acceptable, though at the close of that speech the balance between archaism and colloquialism is very uneasy. Grettir makes the point that the survivors in any age are 'the sly and the dumb'. Cutting across an evocation of hardship and decline comes the music of the world Craven and Ryan endeavoured to escape, where the more real experience is that culled from books, not direct encounter, or else the everyday world is blotted out by the new magic of films.[13]

Grettir is both haunting and haunted. In the saga his fear of the dark is linked with his meeting Glam, a legendary adversary, and his declining fortunes thereafter. At first, when night begins to fall in the 'Eclogue', MacNeice had him asking Craven and Ryan to share his vision: 'Look, do you see his eyes, the idiot glare' (A), but he changed this to something private and sterner, perhaps recollecting the line from *The Choephori* that had struck him some years before ('... I am feeling silly after the Orestia—You don't see them you don't but I see them').[14]

> The dark is falling. Soon the air
> Will stare with eyes, the stubborn ghost
> Who cursed me when I threw him. Must
> The ban go on for ever? I,
> A ghost myself, have no claim now to die.

The eclogue form was particularly suited to an adaptation of Eliot's poetic method, the cutting and swift changes of tone that MacNeice admired. His pleasure in manipulation can be sensed, his delight in the words pelting down with such apparent ease. The counterpoint works well when, with the Voice of Europe as parenthesis, the three speakers move on to spin a litany of dead heroes. The Voice is jazzy—'Always on the dance with an eye to the main / Chance', (the caesura mimicking syncopation)—and nonchalent: 'Who cares / If floods depopulate China?'; while Craven, Ryan, and Grettir give Yeatsian acknowledgements to the boldly individual dead:

> There was MacKenna
> Spent twenty years translating Greek philosophy
> Ill and tormented, unwilling to break contract,
> A brilliant talker who left
> The salon for the solo flight of Mind.[15]

The poem continues as a catalogue of obstacles against which man is urged to go his own way, 'give the voice the lie,/ Outstare the inhuman eyes'. The 'minute gesture' to be made is the adoption of a moral stance: duty is the 'assertion of human values'. Although action is imperative, and the contemporary context in which it must be carried out is made quite explicit by Craven—'Where any day now may see the Gadarene swine / Rush down the gullets of the London tubes / When the enemy, X or Y, let loose their gas'—the possibility of its being political is not even mooted. Hynes's remarks about 'Auden and MacNeice: Their Last Will and Testament' are also applicable to 'Eclogue from Iceland'. He notes that while the poem is riddled with private jokes, the beginning and end are sombre, and the whole is meant seriously: 'What Auden and MacNeice have done is to remove the growing sense of threat from the world of politics, and to place it in the world of morality. It is a significant change of heart.'[16]

Unseriously, the poets proposed a list of beneficiaries for 'Their Last Will', which in the Buffalo notebook is enormous. Not all of them are incorporated in the printed poem, as for instance the conservative bequests to T. S. Eliot, including a Stilton. Besides this collaboration, MacNeice contributed five out of the fifteen sections of Letters from Iceland. Auden's Letter to Lord Byron is clearly the pièce de résistance, but 'Hetty to Nancy' is, as the TLS reviewer said, 'a joyous document' (he suspected Auden to be the author).[17] Indeed most of MacNeice's prose, apart from occasional dull stretches in the pot-boilers, has this verve and precision; it is still evident in his portrait of Dublin, 'Under the Sugar Loaf', and makes one wish he had turned to prose more often.

There is intermittent gaiety in the poem addressed to the Shepards. Son of E. H. Shepard, Graham was one of MacNeice's closest friends at Marlborough and Oxford, sharing his taste for the fantastic and anarchic. 'Letter to Graham and Anna' circles around dilemmas similar to those of the 'Eclogue': the possibility of escape, what is left behind, what is to be salvaged; the distance between the simple past and 'this complex world'. That Iceland did symbolize a real alternative for MacNeice is obvious from the 'Letter'. Lady Nicholson has remarked on his love of the west of Ireland, how he treasured the isolation and would maintain that it was the right place for him to live, and a while later would begin to hanker for the city. Perhaps it would be more accurate to say that Iceland represented a way of living he wished he could settle for:

> Who feed our brains on backchat and self-pity
> And always need a noise, the radio or the city,
> Traffic and changing lights, crashing the amber,
> Always on the move and so do not remember
> The necessity of the silence of the islands,
> The glacier floating in the distance out of existence,

'And there are some who scorn this poésie de départs', but not MacNeice, whose ruminations on the significance of departure and the potential of destinations were clearly associated with the rupture of his marriage. His lines in the 'Letter' on the illusory promise of escape, 'The songs of jazz have told us of a moon country ...', are echoed by the last poem in the 1934-6 Notebook, which in a jazzy way itself creates the mood of the world the MacNeices inhabited in Birmingham, and is explicit about MacNeice's sense of abandonment, 'dizzy with her repercussions/Among striped doors & cups & patch-work cushions'.

Many of the poems in the blue-covered notebook in the Buffalo collection—the earliest manuscripts that can be confidently identified as first drafts—are concerned with the collapse of the MacNeices' marriage. One entitled 'Sonnet' ('You who will soon be unrecapturable ...'), appeared in *Poems* (1937) but was not reprinted. It is typical of the surrounding drafts, with its confident beginning which survives all subsequent changes; then lines altered, deleted, tried again in new combinations; a version settled on in which a couple of lines or groups of words have been telescoped; then the final, often adjectival, emendations. MacNeice rarely changed the length of line, the rhythm, or the general structure once he had set the pattern. When this was established for the longer poems, he seemed to be able to continue indefinitely, as in the draft for 'Eclogue from Iceland'. It was in the process of writing that he discovered where he wanted to go: the deletions do not seem to be after-thoughts, but to be made immediately according to his emerging sense of the poem's structure. The draft of a valedictory poem

to Mary takes up several notebook pages, which suggests that
he was working on it while in Iceland, although the immediate
occasion seems to be packing up house in Birmingham for the
move to Keats Grove, Hampstead. This may have been ac-
complished mainly before the Icelandic trip, as MacNeice did
not return until September, and the term at Bedford College,
where he took up a post as Lecturer in Greek, would have begun
shortly afterwards. Iceland marked the break in his life: the
finish of his marriage, of his first job, of his residence in Birmingham. The poem MacNeice drafted is full of similes for
closure—'a day's play is sealed / & put away in a drawer'—and
becomes the source of lines in *Autumn Journal* (notably in Canto
II) about the kind of life that was ending:

> The past holds on to us. Those who have taken food
> In the sunless kingdom never again make good
> Their escape into the world of sunny crops
> As found Persephone who gaily going up
> Learned that she had been tricked and must return.

It was in this mood of desolation that MacNeice composed a
'Postscript to Iceland: for W. H. Auden' and drew together, as
later in the *Journal*, private and public causes for melancholy.
Three adjacent poems in the collected edition, 'Passage Steamer', 'Postscript' and 'Sand in the Air', use the same stretch of
experience: greyness, monotony of sea or sky, the bleakness of
desertion after the 'fancy turn, you know' (it was at first a
'comic turn'; 'fancy' is flipper). The form of the 'Postscript' is
appropriately Audenesque; 'Sand in the Air' is somewhat
reminiscent of Auden's song 'Stop all the clocks, cut off the
telephone'. 'Postscript' is a long fuse of fear: 'down in Europe
Seville fell' and the Aryan Olympics were run; the city closes
in with the approach of winter and a return to interpreting
dead books:

> Through that forest of dead words
> I would hunt the living birds—
>
> Great black birds that fly alone
> Slowly through a land of stone,
> And the gulls who weave a free
> Quilt of rhythm on the sea.

A set of birds different from those in 'Passage Steamer', who 'insinuate that nothing we pass is past, / That all our beginnings were long since begun'. Fear of 'loneliness / And uncommunicableness'—the very clumsiness of the word attesting to obstacles—operates on the personal level and by implication, dangerously, on the public one; the fuse ignites in the last stanza:

> Our prerogatives as men
> Will be cancelled who knows when;
> Still I drink your health before
> The gun-butt raps upon the door.

This has the air of an earlier world of Auden's, the arena of missions and trials of strength, unknown destinations and dangers. But it is not the stuff of legend nor, as Hynes points out, of melodrama. That year the poet Lorca was killed and, in other circumstances, John Cornford. MacNeice had met Cornford once, as a hitch-hiker, and had written to Blunt with uncharacteristic enthusiasm: '... obviously he is the one chap of the whole damn lot of you who is going to be a great man. There is still hope for the human race.'[18] Referring to the stanza quoted above, as well as Auden's 'I'm home to Europe where I may be shot', Hynes concludes that: 'these passages render images of a possible reality that had not existed for earlier English writers; as the end of the decade approached, the alien and frightful violence of *The Brown Book of the Hitler Terror* was becoming domesticated in English imaginations' (p. 292).

One of the most famous poems of the period, distinctly more insouciant than any of the Icelandic ones, was MacNeice's 'Bagpipe Music'. Having already been slipped into *Poems* (1937) published by Random House, it first appeared in England in *New Verse*, January 1938. In his copy, Geoffrey Grigson noted beside 'Bagpipe Music': 'A poem refused by *The Listener* as indelicate'.[19]

There is a recording of MacNeice reading a selection of his poems, made in 1961; 'Bagpipe Music' is the light relief ending the first side.[20] His prefatory remarks are adapted from his commentary on the record sleeve. MacNeice sees the poem in the context of the Munich year, though anticipating it; like

'The Sunlight on the Garden' 'very must of its period in that it
is permeated with a sense of imminent doom in the outer
world'. On the surface, it is 'a nonsense poem and a piece of
technical fun and games (the bad feminine rhymes are meant
to suggest the wheeze of the pipes)', underneath it is 'a satirical
elegy for the Gaelic districts of Scotland and indeed for all
traditional culture'. MacNeice's reading of the poem is a
raspingly vigorous performance, gathering speed as it goes,
ending on an up-beat. W. T. McKinnon detects the 'skirling
rhythms of the reel (predominant iambs and trochees) interwoven with the slower trisyllabic rhythms of the strathspey';
to such rhythmic virtuosity MacNeice adds ingenious rhymes—
'... it's no-go Blavatsky / ... a bit of skirt in a taxi'—and sophisticated yet accessible wit.[21] The poem connects precisely with
contemporary life, from 'their knickers are made of crêpe-de-
chine' to Willie Murray's brother who 'went upon the parish',
using facts that were really painful with the awareness that
playing with them removed the sting, yet mocked the player's
attempts.

In a period dominated by Auden, MacNeice's verse showed
remarkably little trace of his influence. Auden's use of ballads
had been anticipated by Yeats; MacNeice commended both for
their compromise with tradition: '... the poet achieves some of
the simplicity or directness or swing of the primitive form but
he does not pretend away ... his own sophisticated self' (*Yeats*,
p. 149). His own 'Laredo' was to be a powerful example of
such compromise. The distinctive tone of Auden's poetry,
confident and at ease with abstractions (Love, History), was
based on the assumption that a pattern could be imposed on
the diverse elements a poem might include. MacNeice, despite
his conviction that a poet is a shaper, doubted the validity of
the exercise. He consistently praised Auden, however, and not
least for his 'return to a versification in more regular stanzas
and rhymes'.[22] Yet it was out of 'the least valuable elements in
Auden', as F. O. Matthiessen remarked, that MacNeice constructed his one monument to his contemporary, the play *Out of
the Picture*.[23]

MacNeice had tried his hand at plays twice before. At
Birmingham the University Dramatic Society produced his
Station Bell to round off a term, and the Group Theatre acted

his translation of the *Agamemnon* in November 1936. He wrote
to Blunt about the former: 'My play is still unfinished—so
protean—but I hope it will be done in London by a thing
called, I think, the Group Theatre. I am afraid it wouldn't be
allowed in the I.F.S. as De Val. wld take it personally. It will
look very well on the boards.'[24] It was a satirical farce about a
future Ireland under a very topical dictator and an Irish brand
of Fascism. The dictator is a woman, Julia, and part of the
play concerns her relationship with her unaggressive husband.
A feeling of unreality pervades the work, particularly the chaotic
ending involving men dressed as giants.

When MacNeice approached T. S. Eliot about publishing
the *Agamemnon* translation, he put in a word for a play of his
own, then called *The Rising Venus*.[25] He had mentioned it some-
time before to Rupert Doone, referring to the 'Irishness' of an
unnamed play, presumably *Station Bell*, and saying that he was
writing another which would be less of a compromise between
two traditions. MacNeice articulated his theoretical position in
a 'Dialogue on the necessity for an active tradition and experiment', which he and Doone spoke in the Group Theatre rooms
on 22 November 1936, and later in an article 'The Play and the
Audience', contributed to a symposium.[26]

In the Group Theatre dialogue, MacNeice argued for an
essentially Aristotelian version of tragedy, centring on the idea
that a play should be an 'organic unity'. He admired Yeats's
effort to revive poetic drama, but maintained that his values
were anachronistic and that the verse itself was 'too obviously
traditional in style'. Nevertheless he found Yeats's theorizing
valuable in its reaction away from character, its emphasis on
ideas, plot, and poetry. MacNeice suggested that Eliot in
Murder in the Cathedral and Auden in *The Ascent of F6* corroborated
the theory in practice. 'We go to a play to see the bold patterns
of life stripped of the ivy and creepers of personal idiosyncrasies.
This was so in Greek tragedy. The main pattern of the play
will of course be very greatly brought out and reinforced by the
producer.' This nod in Doone's direction would not have been
entirely reverent: to MacNeice's anxiety over the *Agamemnon*'s
being static, Doone's response was, 'I am dynamic, so fuck
all.'[27] His proposal to have Cassandra 'gibbering unseen in a
sort of portable bathing tent', as MacNeice described it, was

fortunately eliminated during rehearsal, but on the first night
the Chorus were still dressed in dinner-jackets. Dodds felt that
in the general attempt to prove Aeschylus 'relevant', Doone
had made a 'dreadful hash', and did not wonder at Yeats's
comment that they were assisting at the death of tragedy. Still,
the dinner-jacket detail must have impressed at least one
member of the audience: T. S. Eliot originally planned to have
the Furies in *The Family Reunion* dressed likewise.

Agamemnon was better received than *Out of the Picture,* though
the latter was undoubtedly more suited to the Group Theatre
style. It was a play that nearly conformed to the credo Mac-
Neice set out in the symposium:

> I think that plays should be written about the important problems which fill
> the lives of nations and individuals. ... Plays on generalised subjects should
> probably be written by poets, using probably some non-naturalistic technique.
> ... Belief and rhythm—the two things least evident in our modern theatre—
> are the two things most to be desired in it. (*Footnotes*, p. 42)

By 'important problems' MacNeice did not intend political
ones, indeed in the same article he wrote contemptuously of
what was passed off as theatre because of its political content,
by playwrights catering to a clique; he mentioned particularly
'the aegis of Mr Victor Gollancz and the shadow of Spain'.
Out of the Picture has two plot levels: one is the fairly complicated
life of a portrait-painter, Portwright, and Moll O'Hara (the
model for his picture 'Venus Rising'), which intersects with
that of Clara de Groot, a film star who is being incompetently
analysed by Dr Spielmann; the other is the slow advance of
war. Portweight and Moll plainly represent the life-giving
powers of art, but they cannot stand against the life-denying,
inhuman forces which grind on despite Portwright's killing
the Minister of 'Peace'.

The mechanistic progress of destruction is conveyed by
means of a Radio Announcer, and a Listener, who close most
of the scenes of the first act. While this renders the war both
remote and inexorable, it is a clumsy device at times, as in the
whisky-fuelled declamation of the section entitled 'Les neiges
d'antan' in *Collected Poems*. A chorus (off) takes over with lines
of urban apocalypse, shouting 'FIRE' at intervals in mock-
Eliot fashion.

A further echo of Eliot is found in 'The jingles of the morning', MacNeice's paean to the commonplace joys that will disappear with the war:

> Shall we remember the games with puffball and
>   plantain,
> Searching for the lost handle to the silent fountain,
> Hiding in the shrubbery, shutting our eyes and
>   counting?

Burnt Norton was published in April 1936; *Out of the Picture* sent to Faber's in June of the same year.

The elegaic mood already present in *Letters from Iceland,* and at its finest in *Autumn Journal,* was peculiarly suited to MacNeice's temperament: it even crept into his literary criticism in 1938. *Modern Poetry,* despite all the signs of revival MacNeice found in Auden and his contemporaries, was written in the shadow of crisis, in the expectation that poetry might 'for the time be degraded or even silenced' (p. 205). This 'plea for *impure* poetry, that is, for poetry conditioned by the poet's life and the world around him' (Preface), was concerned with the anatomizing of that life, in terms of taste and intellect, as well as analysis of his generation's poetry. MacNeice has been unfairly subsumed in 'Macspaunday', a myth perpetuated in part by his own book. Randall Jarrell noted in the *Kenyon Review* that MacNeice's having to bracket Spender with Auden, out of modesty not calling attention to his own work, led to a certain weakness in his examples.[28]

MacNeice produced 'My Case-Book' because he believed that personal factors were vital in determining what was written, but these were themselves offered as typical of his class, background, and age, which he held in common with most of his literary peers. The result of this post-Great War conditioning was a change of attitude among the poets: they would take sides on issues, make an emotional stand; and they would make form more flexible to match altered circumstances, even simplify reality if necessary. Thus the break between Auden and Eliot: although MacNeice himself is quick to say that moving away from an aesthetic or mystical view of poetry, taking greater account of the material world in which he moves, must not blind the poet to human sympathies, or render his world-picture crudely coloured.

The insistence in *Modern Poetry* is above all on poetry as a non-specialized activity, almost a natural overflow from conversation, and correspondingly on the poet as a man wholly alert, but not essentially different from other men. The conclusion of the book contains the nub of MacNeice's contentions, his much quoted ideal of a poet, who is:

a blend of the entertainer and the critic or informer; he is not a legislator ... nor yet, essentially, a prophet. ... His object is ... to record a fact *plus and therefore modified* by his own emotional reaction to it; ...
... I would have a poet able-bodied, fond of talking, a reader of the newspapers, capable of pity and laughter, informed in economics, appreciative of women, involved in personal relationships, actively interested in politics, susceptible to physical impressions. (pp. 197-8)

This characterization inescapably set the pattern for criticism of MacNeice: it accounted for many facets of his own personality and it was in the spirit of the decade, if belatedly, in rendering the artist more accessible to his public. What poetry added to life, MacNeice went on to say, often consisted 'merely in the illumination of that public's own experience' (p. 200).

However limited as a definition, it did provide the critical rationale for *Autumn Journal*, as Walter Allen points out in his introduction to the 1968 edition of *Modern Poetry*. The poem is generally considered to have captured the mood of the Munich weeks more successfully than any contemporary writing: '... he put a lot of day to day living, almost journalism, into it, and yet the total effect is that of a complete phase of the thirties, the post-Munich depression one might call it, absolutely realised and felt in every line of the poem, even when it's about something else ...'.[29] Disappointingly, there are no traces of drafts, emended copies, or notes for the *Journal* in any available collection. MacNeice perhaps did not consider them worth preserving, and after his marriage broke up led an unsettled life not conducive to conservation. One suspects anyway that many of the thirties' poems were not heavily worked over. Talking about the years in which she knew him best (*c.*1936-9), Nancy Sharp commented:

In those days Louis was warm and expansive and gay, he wrote poetry most of the time. He used to slip an envelope over to me sometimes across the table, and on the back of it was scribbled a new poem. This was tremendously exciting. He talked to me about his poetry sometimes, and I remember him telling me he was writing a poem on the British Museum Reading Room. I was unimpressed and he mocked me. 'You think poems should always be about life and death, don't you? Well, I don't.' (*Radio Portrait*, p. 13)

Ernst Stahl, recalling MacNeice's periods of creativity 'over the years in unexpected places', remembered that 'he wrote a section of *Autumn Journal* in a Paris bar'.[30] The only, and scarcely telling, hint is a comment in a letter to Eliot (4 October 1937) to the effect that MacNeice was considering writing a book about his experience teaching Classics—and learning them at Marlborough and Oxford—some of which, he thought, could be in verse.

Besides the explanatory note prefacing the poem, MacNeice provided one extensive gloss on his intentions. This was attached to a brief letter to Eliot (22 November 1938) and was to be the basis for the relevant entry in Faber's Spring Catalogue.

Autumn Journal:

A long poem from 2,000 to 3,000 lines written from August to December 1938. Not strictly a journal but giving the tenor of my intellectual and emotional experiences during that period.

It is about nearly everything which from firsthand experience I consider significant.

It is written in sections averaging about 80 lines in length. This division gives it a *dramatic* quality, as different parts of myself (e.g. the anarchist, the defeatist, the sensual man, the philosopher, the would-be good citizen) can be given their say in turn.

It contains rapportage, metaphysics, ethics, lyrical emotion, autobiography, nightmare.

There is constant interrelation of abstract and concrete. Generalizations balanced by pictures. ...

It is written throughout in an elastic kind of quatrain. This form a) gives the whole poem a formal unity but b) saves it from monotony by allowing it a great range of appropriate variations. ...

I think this is my best work to date, it is both a panorama and a confession of faith.

A poem elastic enough to include all the above has of course earned criticism, summed up by John Lehmann: '... rambling, facile, prosy at times, never very deep or certain in thought, rather too conspicuously elaborating the picture of an easygoing but attractive personality.'[31] On the contrary, the poem does have a discernible structure and movement; its verbal ease, though sometimes self-indulgent, has precision as well as

facility; the thought is of necessity uncertain, and does not set
out to be profound; the personality emerges as attractive, but
primarily troubled and diffident. MacNeice liked Baudelaire's
comment that he had tried, 'plus d'une fois, comme tous mes
amis, de m'enformer dans un système pour y prêcher à mon
aise. Mais un système est une espèce de damnation... Je suis
revenu chercher un asile dans l'impeccable naïveté.' Delmore
Schwartz, in his intelligent review of *Poems* (1935), calls Mac-
Neice's way of handling his material 'adroitly naïve', approving of his ability to move from general statements and wide
references to direct impressions, tangible sensations. The
journal form was exactly the way to avoid system, to encompass
everyday life, political commentary, philosophical excursions,
the structure being provided by the passing months: 'the cir-
cumference is always social and the centre is always personal'.[32]

Both eclogue and journal indulged MacNeice's penchant for
writing in the contemporary idiom as well as about the current
crises. His fondness for using and twisting clichés led him to
banality sometimes, at others he achieved the intended quality
of surprise. Perhaps this style had its literary sanction in the
Latin poets, whose use of similes and allusions MacNeice
defended as being the main point of the poem, not just decor-
ation; '... the apparent theme is the mere occasion for the birth
of something new, something achieved through the redeploying
and reshuffling of myths or images or, as often with these
Romans, clichés' ('Images', p. 124). It was the linguistic equi-
valent of his subject-matter, both veering away from obscurity
and esotericism.

Most of the *Journal*'s concerns are broached in the opening
canto: the life of the secure bourgeois, the potential for its being
undermined, the life of other classes—the poem is very conscious of social hierarchy—, and the feeling for endings: end of
a season, of one way of living, of a marriage; all the old dis-
pensations going. There is also a pervasive sense of movement,
of urban rhythm. Although there are glimpses of the countryside, they are usually caught from moving vehicles. MacNeice
sees domesticated nature, city parks, and well-kept gardens.

In the first section of *Autumn Journal* there is the faintest
evocation of the summer before the last war, remembered as
the most brilliant in years:

Close and slow, summer is ending in Hampshire,
  Ebbing away down ramps of shaven lawn where
    close-clipped yew
Insulates the lives of retired generals and admirals
  And the spyglasses hung in the hall and the
    prayer-books ready in the pew
And August going out to the tin trumpets of
  nasturtiums

This was not an imagined but a real scene: according to Lady Nicholson, MacNeice and his family stayed with Lady Lowry (his step-aunt, widow of an admiral) at Wickham, Hampshire in 1938. All the 'inherited assets of bodily ease' were thus known to him, but as an importation from his stepmother's comfortably established family rather than as part of his early life. Clearly the setting takes on the character of its inhabitants, washed up and beached since the Great War, their beliefs, it is implied, outdated as their equipment, or futile now as then; military splendour as menacing as flowers. MacNeice embalms it in a phrase later in the canto, 'All quiet on the Family Front', in a world where only rolling stock disappears 'Into poppy sidings for the night—night which knows no passion / No assault of hands or tongue'. Thus the parallel theme of loneliness, in particular sexual loneliness, is introduced, not yet elaborated although picked up again with the mention of 'My dog, a symbol of the abandoned order'. The section closes with MacNeice's arrival in London: 'West Meon, Tisted, Farnham, Woking, Weybridge, / Then London's packed and stale and pregnant air'.[33]

The recurrent cantos of philosophizing are probably the least strong elements of the poem, but they are not inessential. II and III are concerned with the difficulties of continuing, the necessity for change, the hankering for the past and stability in both private and public spheres. The temptation to oblivion, 'pure Not-Being, Nirvana', is weighed against the thought that 'Becoming is a match for Being': MacNeice as indulgent solipsist against MacNeice who wishes to bear witness to 'the human animal's endless courage', to align himself with the others. They are also returning at the end of August, taking up old lives, routines of work and solace. He may have borne in mind

the thirtieth poem in Auden's *Look Stranger* (1936), the birthday
poem to Isherwood which opens 'August for the people and
their favourite islands', and contains the lines:

> So in this hour of crisis and dismay,
> What better than your strict and adult pen
> Can warn us from the colours and the consolations,
> The showy arid works, reveal
> The squalid shadow of academy and garden,
> Make action urgent and its nature clear?

MacNeice implies that this is not only the novelist's but also
the poet's dilemma, and considers the position of an apolitical,
or at least non-aligned, intellectual faced with the possibility of
action. He had engaged in the same debate in *I Crossed the
Minch* (an account of a trip to the Hebrides) with a censorious
Guardian Angel who doubted the extent of his political commitment:

My sympathies are Left. On paper and in the soul. But not in my heart or my
guts. On paper—yes. I would vote Left any day, sign manifestos, answer
questionnaires. Ditto, my soul. My soul is all for moving towards the classless
society. But unlike Plato, what my soul says does not seem to go. ... With my
heart and my guts I lament the passing of class. (pp. 125, 127)

In *Autumn Journal* he is more willing to take the Angel's part,
yet the main impression is of a being divided. This was written
at a time other intellectuals, who had readily espoused the
proletariat cause, were beginning to waver. Few who had made
their avowals publicly now publicly disavowed their stance, it
was just a quiet drift. While MacNeice's position may not have
been entirely admirable, his admission of it and puzzled fidelity
to it have their own courage. In Canto III, there is still room
for hope, for change on a personal scale at least:

> But may I cure that habit, look up and outwards
> And may my feet follow my wider glance
> First no doubt to stumble, then to walk with the
>   others
> And in the end—with time and luck—to dance.

This takes us naturally into Canto IV's homage to a woman,
since MacNeice always associates the beloved with an ability to
give life pattern and rhythm. It is in memory of an affair al-

ready over, 'all of London littered with remembered kisses'. The images match some employed in 'Leaving Barra'; the woman 'whose hair is twined in all my waterfalls' is likely to be Nancy Sharp, who accompanied MacNeice on the Hebridean trip (she illustrated the book, and *Zoo*). Her 'words would tumble over each other and pelt / From pure excitement', a description sometimes appropriate to his own poetic style, where the choice of words and their combination seem fortunately hit upon rather than inherently exact. The canto's elation, the recognition of distinctive qualities in people and objects to which she alerted him, sweeps him into V, which is concerned no longer with memory but with menace.[34] It is the first of MacNeice's many London poems; each impression is sharpened by anxiety—'Hodza, Henlein, Hitler' replace the cricket score as the 'latest'—everything named may be destroyed:

> Nelson is stone and Johnnie Walker moves his
>   Legs like a cretin over Trafalgar Square.
> And in the Corner House the carpet-sweepers
>   Advance between the tables after crumbs
> Inexorably, like a tank battalion
>   In answer to the drums.

This is the strategy of Canto I, unease created by the insertion of military images into domesticity. The old literary game of the thirties, with spies, tests, and, above all, frontiers, drops its guise of play: 'The bloody frontier / Converges on our beds'. For MacNeice, going home does not obscure the fraying edges, it emphasizes them.

The transition from troubled sleep in London (V) to Spain (VI) is facilitated by a reminder of Auden's phrase, 'But today the struggle', from 'Spain'. Looking back on his trip to the country with Blunt, it is the Spain of literary/artistic imagination that MacNeice evokes, seen through the rain by a disgruntled tourist, noticing the 'fretted stone the Moor / Had chiselled for effects of sun and shadow', realizing painfully in 1938 that

> ... only an inch behind
>   This map of olive and ilex, this painted hoarding;
> Careless of visitors the people's mind
>   Was tunnelling like a mole to day and danger.

Connolly thought that MacNeice was more balanced than either Auden or Spender in his attitude to the Civil War: '... he kept his head. He was of course anti-Franco but somehow he wasn't ever one of those bogus hunger-marchers that some people become too easily' (*Radio Portrait*, C.t.). From all the early Civil War writing at least, the conviction emerges that this was a simple contest between Right and Wrong. Such emotional assent is comprehensible, if at odds with the retrospective view that an imposition of foreign objectives on the Spanish struggle made the cause as complex as any. For many intellectuals it was not only a show-down between Fascism and Democracy, but also a clear polarization of forces at work in British society. The theme of England in Spain runs through the poetry: Auden declared that 'the struggle in Spain has x-rayed the lies on which our civilization is built'. MacNeice gave it most memorable expression at the close of Canto VI; they departed from La Linea

> ... not realising
> That Spain would soon denote
>   Our grief, our aspirations;
> Not knowing that our blunt
>   Ideals would find their whetstone, that our spirit
> Would find its frontier on the Spanish front,
>   Its body in a rag-tag army.

This and Canto VII are full of the world of newspaper events, the atmosphere of preparation: 'They are cutting down the trees on Primrose Hill. / The wood is white like the roast flesh of chicken'; the simile is an example of his ability to draw on a fund of homely images, a strength MacNeice admired in Herbert. Here it evokes the threatened Sunday traditions, roasts and leisure, an end to 'the old régime'. The private order that has vanished for MacNeice is described in the following canto: the sensuous carelessness of the first years of marriage in Birmingham, the companionship, the isolation from others' worries that it is part of the *Journal*'s business to break down.

The resumption of routine after Munich ('only the Czechs / Go down and without fighting') meant for MacNeice returning to his role 'As impresario of the Ancient Greeks'. The Argo

selection includes his reading Canto IX, of which he says:
'... far from being objective about the Ancient Greeks, I see
them here in the light of the mood induced in me by Munich'.
Connolly noted that 'although he loved the classics, he didn't
get stuck in that English Hellenistic mould' (*Radio Portrait*,
C.t.). Allowed their intellectual graces at the beginning of the
canto, the Greeks degenerate as it proceeds, slipping into the
same factional and double-crossing political games that com-
prised the policies of the thirties.

This consideration leads back naturally to MacNeice's
schooling in the classics, to nostalgia for and criticism of Marlborough and Sherborne. 'Generalizations balanced by pictures
... ': the technique works within cantos and from one to the
next; from details of school years to statements about what was
gained, and on to emotional education: 'I am harassed by
familiar devils, / By those I cannot see, by those I may not
touch', an adaptation of a line in *The Choephori* encountered in
his formal education. Canto XI is for his former wife, admitting
her faults but wistful for a woman whose 'instinct sanctions' all
she does. The balance in his worldly judgements praised by
Connolly is here implied to be a liability, in coping with or
matching her 'whose kaleidoscopic ways are all authentic, /
Whose truth is not of a statement but of a dance'.

The endings of most of the cantos are muted and XI though
avowing content is passive, its tone carrying over into XII:
'These days are misty, insulated, mute / ... And we hardly
have the heart to meddle / Any more with personal epics or ·
public calls'. 'Roman weather', MacNeice calls it, threading
philosophy with a childhood memory of 'the sergeant barking
at bayonet practice', when troops were stationed at Carrickfergus in the First World War. Between Aristotle and Plato he
had for a long time chosen the 'biologist', feeling more com-
fortable with Aristotle's stress on 'function', intermittently able
to find the reality of himself in his function as poet when other
touchstones seemed to disappear.[35]

MacNeice states his ideal modestly enough in this canto:

> All that I would like to be is human, having a share
> In a civilised, articulate and well-adjusted
> Community where the mind is given its due
> But the body is not distrusted.

On the one hand, education past a certain level encourages conformity, a desire for safety; on the other, 'If it were not for Lit. Hum. I might be climbing / A ladder with a hod.' The analysis of Lit. Hum. proves to be one of the best cantos in the poem (XIII). It carries both the intellectual excitement of the course and a cool puncturing of its pretensions; it has the arrogance of the classical student 'bred to the purple', who, Connolly remarked, 'could be inclined to make other people feel they hadn't got these Firsts', while it mocks that attitude (*Radio Portrait*, p. 9). 'That the actual was not real and the real was not with us / And that all that mattered was the One' was a concept with which it was fun to play, but it did not win MacNeice's allegiance. Writing later of the same period, he was more serious about his predilection for Nietzsche, the German idealists, his flirtation with Schopenhauer:

Having been brought up in a traditionally religious family, and having, true to my period, reacted violently against the Christian dogma and, to some extent too, against the Christian ethic, I felt morally naked and spiritually hungry. So I was tempted to experiment simultaneously with two very different types of cure or defence—the Gallic grain of salt ... and the hidden magic of the Rheingold. Let everything be either vanity or One! It was to take me some time to close for a middle way. ('When I was Twenty-One', p. 232)

Whereas Oxford had not fostered any political awareness during his undergraduate years, the by-election there in October 1938 was controversial enough for MacNeice to be 'Driving voters to the polls / In that home of lost illusions'.

Quinton Hogg, son of the Lord Chancellor and a university contemporary of MacNeice's, was defending the seat specifically on the issue of foreign policy and the Munich Agreement; against him stood A. D. Lindsay, the Master of Balliol. Hogg's majority was almost halved but he retained the seat. MacNeice came away in a mood that recalled the warning he had put in Grettir's mouth: 'Each occasion must be used, however trivial'.

> The nicest people in England have always been the least
> Apt to solidarity or alignment
> But all of them must now align against the beast
> That prowls at every door and barks in every headline.

It is an old mood he recaptures too in the nightmare canto, the desire to turn his back on the menace, to blot it out with drink and companionship. There is desperation in the nearly incoherent, quickly succeeding phrases, snatches of nursery rhyme, proverbs, philosophy; everything uselessly heaped up to keep the real knowledge out, though it is solidly there at the close. The predicament is that voiced in 'Wolves', now shared by a whole community.

Real violence had been present in MacNeice's life long before the thirties, in the actions of his intransigent countrymen, whom he attacks in Canto XVI with some virulence. His emotion almost takes him by surprise: 'I thought I was well / Out of it, educated and domiciled in England'. The undesired strength of Ireland's attraction provides the canto's tension, and fuels its dismissive fury, to which there can be no sequel. XVII is a philosophical meditation from the bath, as though such leisurely theorizing is a way of immunization against futile anger. Yet the cantos are connected in that MacNeice is exploring in both possibilities of community and division; in XVI in a national context, in XVII on a personal level, making the difficult admission that 'other people are always / Organic to the self, that a monologue / Is the death of language'.

The next four cantos are governed by their month, December. It is a time for taking stock and for peering into the new year, pessimistic activities. The 'seeds of energy and choice' (XVIII) are barely noted, what persists is fear for the future, England diminished in the present, everything shadowed, rebirth an illusion. Christmas was associated with his wife and she is gone, he now acknowledges, without hope of return. Not only the old philosophies—Christian or humanist—mock, but also the old masters: 'The unfounded confidence of the dead affronts / Our own system of values' (XX). MacNeice, who sees 'the quiet hands seduce / Of the god who is god of nothing', who can appeal to no established system of belief, manages to resist the temptation to make the great refusal, and he couches this resistance in contemporary terms: 'I feel that such a defeat is also treason, / That deaths like these are also lies' (XXI).

This densely interwoven poem of public and personal life does not end without its affirmations, tentative or speculative though they may be. In December as the first snow fell on

London (with its still embattled air: 'At night we sleep behind stockades of frost'), MacNeice ran south, via Paris, where he absorbed the 'tourist values' and longed for flirtation. If the tourist stance towards Spain had been knowledgeably abandoned, what took its place for the committed intelligentsia was really only a variant: the trips followed by reports in the *New Statesman, Spectator*, and *Left Review* of the Spaniards' courage, the feeling of solidarity, the urgency of the case for British intervention. Such accounts left out much of what was discouraging about the Civil War, notably the bloody division among the Communists: 'these people contain truth, whatever / Their nominal façade' (XXIII).

By the time *Autumn Journal* was published, Barcelona had fallen and the Loyalists were defeated. But on this New Year's Eve, they prompted MacNeice to shame and a harsh assessment of himself and those who had joined him in self-pity, 'the fun of cursing the wicked / World into which we were born / And the cynical admission of frustration'. He proclaimed in his *Spectator* article that 'it is impossible to be a Hamlet in Barcelona'.[36] The end of a year and an era was an end, also, to poses:

> I have loved defeat and sloth,
>   The tawdry halo of the idle martyr;
> I have thrown away the roots of will and conscience,
>   Now I must look for both,
> Not any longer act among the cushions
>   The Dying Gaul;

MacNeice had no programme of action to offer: solutions are not usually the province of journals. It is only in fiction that a shape can be given, a real end imposed; or in loose narrative poetry such as Clough's *Amours de Voyage*, which surely Mac-Neice knew and must have admired for its play of doomed personal relations (and successful or amusing ones) against tumultuous political events, for its flexible versifying and modulation of tone. Like Horace, whose poetry greatly influenced his own, MacNeice did not have a primarily didactic intention; like him, he wished to operate rationally and conducted much of his attack by means of debate. Horace's *Satires* and MacNeice's *Journal* are permeated by political disenchantment, are bereft of religious hope, and sceptical—MacNeice less so—of the nature of personal relations. They also share stylistic affinities: ease, neatness, rapidity; MacNeice perhaps lacks Horace's elegance, but does attain a lyricism unsuited to the *Satires*.

He closes *Autumn Journal* with a dismissal of his doubt, a lullaby for the people he loves, in acceptance that takes its strength from all that has gone before. It is not exactly hopeful, but MacNeice's mood is resolute:

> Sleep to the noise of running water
>   To-morrow to be crossed, however deep;
> This is no river of the dead or Lethe,
>   To-night we sleep
> On the banks of the Rubicon—the die is cast;
>   There will be time to audit
> The accounts later, there will be sunlight later
>   And the equation will come out at last.

III. AN END TO NOSTALGIA?

> But just seeing things is a tourist activity; a poet is allowed
> to be a tourist just as he is allowed to be a journalist—but
> only so long as it satisfies him. After *The Earth Compels*
> I tired of tourism and after *Autumn Journal* I tired of jour-
> nalism.[1]

With the War came a discernible, if gradual, change in Mac-
Neice's poetry. The 1930s had seen a rash of books, witness to
financial pressure and a compulsion towards self-definition:
Zoo and the travel books are full of personal asides, entirely
subjective digressions that have little bearing on the ostensible
objects of writing. The culmination of self-exploration was
reached in *The Strings Are False*, which MacNeice outlined,
although not under that title, in a letter to Eliot in September
1939, when reminiscence seemed a vital act of preservation.
Only manuscript drafts of the autobiography survived, Dodds
as literary executor deftly editing them for posthumous publication.

MacNeice also felt challenged to provide a defence of the
kind of poetry he and his contemporaries had produced in the
previous decade. It was attacked by Virginia Woolf in a paper
read to the Workers' Educational Association in Brighton in
May 1940, which was published in *Folios of New Writing* in the
autumn of that year. MacNeice's reply, with those of Edward
Upward, B. L. Coombes, and John Lehmann, appeared in
Folios for spring 1941 (pp. 37-41). Although he did not refer to
it specifically, Woolf had quoted quite extensively from *Autumn
Journal*, which she thought 'feeble as poetry but interesting as
autobiography'.[2]

Woolf gave a brief sketch of nineteenth-century writing
conditions, persisting until the abyss of the Great War. She
looked at education, saw the influence of public and private
schools, of Oxbridge, and concluded that the writer had been
sitting upon 'a tower raised above the rest of us; a tower built
first on his parents' station, then on his parents' gold' (*Essays*,
p. 169). The 'us' was somewhat disingenuous: despite her lack
of university education, Virginia Woolf was also firmly seated.
After 1918, this secure tower had begun to lean, under the

pressure of war and continual social upheaval, and to lean leftwards. Elevated by the same means as their predecessors, writers were nevertheless victims of consciousness: of self, class, change, falling, and the imminence of death. Circumstances sent them back to the only stability they could discern, themselves: 'they have been great egotists' (p. 177). Circumstances forced them to be politicians, as 'Mr MacNeice bears witness', compelled them 'to preach, if not by their living, at least by their writing, the creation of a society in which everyone is equal and everyone is free' (p. 175). Woolf argued that, having no knowledge of a 'towerless' society, after their destruction of the present bourgeois one—from which they had benefited—the thirties' writers offered nothing to put in its place.

This was her weakest line and MacNeice exposed it in his reply, defending didacticism as the inevitable response to the world she herself admitted to be chaotic, and full of evils needing to be stigmatized. He explained and diluted the Marxist connection: '... some at least of these poets—in particular Auden and Spender—always recognised the truth of Thomas Mann's dictum: "Karl Marx must read Friedrich Hölderlin"' (Folios, p.40). But the main tenor of his defence is intuitive: Auden and Spender brought 'a new spirit of hopefulness' into English poetry; 'my generation at least put some salt in it' (p. 41). He concluded defensively, with none of the elegant rhetoric of Woolf's attack:

We may not have done all we could in the Thirties, but we did do something. We were right to have thrown mud at Mrs Woolf's old horses and we were right to advocate social reconstruction and we were even right—in our more lyrical work—to give personal expression to our feelings of anxiety, horror and despair (for even despair can be fertile).

The tone is of a man firmly, if resignedly, packing away the past. Yet it could not be so simple, as MacNeice realized: 'Recantation is becoming too fashionable; I am sorry to see so much self-flagellation, so many Peccavis, going on on the literary Left.'[3] It is perhaps not surprising that MacNeice's prose in the 1940s, particularly during the War, is greatly occupied with moral and ethical issues, with the skeleton of belief necessary to the body of art. The idealism of the thirties persisted; the form it took was an insistence on the value of community, and on the inclusiveness to which art could attain.

In this decade, as in the previous, tumultous public events were matched by devastating personal experiences. MacNeice had visited America for the first time in the spring of 1939, and in the course of his lecturing had met 'someone whom according to fairy story logic I was bound to meet but according to common sense never. A women who was not a destroyer' (*Strings*, p. 204). By the autumn of that year he was in Ireland, applying for the Chair of English at Trinity College Dublin, and unsure about his role in the War: '... I think of plumping for something brainless. There must be plenty of people to propagand so I have no feeling of guilt in refusing to mortify my mind.'[4] He returned briefly to England in January 1940 before setting out for America once more, this time to teach at Cornell. It looked to some as though he were emigrating in the wake of Auden and Isherwood, whose departure for the USA in January 1939 Cyril Connolly had labelled 'the most important literary event since the outbreak of the Spanish War'.[5] He may be the third writer in Christopher Lee's poem, emotively titled 'Trahison des Clercs':

> One sailed for New York: a second followed;
> one at that moment broke his heart for a woman,
> showing the pieces to strangers in cafés,
> making of the world's calamity
> a mirror of his own sensitiveness; ...
> But what of us
> remaining, so perplexed:
> shall we still honour poets of the people, look
> for wisdom in their words, or vexed
> watch down the wind these swift migrating birds?[6]

Although peritonitis and convalescence detained MacNeice in America, and his love for Eleanor Clark must have inclined him to stay, in December 1940 he was back in London. He attempted to join the Royal Navy and was rejected on medical grounds. Propaganda was to be his fate after all: he joined the BBC Features Department in May 1941. 1942 held three important events: the death of Bishop MacNeice, marriage to the singer Hedli Anderson, and the death of Graham Shepard.

At the outbreak of the Second World War, then, MacNeice was in Ireland on a journey he had planned with Ernst Stahl:

'... the fatalist within me said, "War or no war, you have got to go back to the West. If only for a week. Because you may never again.'" [7] This time it was not the Ireland of his childhood that his poetry evoked; the quality of menace and nightmare arises not from the imagination but from real events, a flight dogged by radio bulletins. The poems that make up *The Last Ditch* (1940) are filled with futile anger, nostalgia, longing: for Ireland, for America, for Eleanor Clark (to whom the volume is dedicated), for the certainly disappearing world MacNeice had known. The fact that the book was brought out by the Cuala Press, run by Yeats's sisters in Dublin, 'somehow tied MacNeice up with the Irish movement in a way that his other books of poems hadn't ever done', Connolly remarked (*Radio Portrait*, C.t.). In this sense too it was 'the closing album'; he could no longer go back and forth to Ireland, and during the Blitz his identification with London life was powerfully re-inforced.

'Dublin' is a much less bitter poem than might have been expected in the aftermath of the Irish canto of *Autumn Journal*, its perspective undoubtedly softened by the apparent finality of the farewells MacNeice was making. Yet he does not lose sight of the extraordinary Dublin combination of a famished remnant with all to which Ascendancy pride laid claim, 'the bare bones of a fanlight / Over a hungry door'. His own feeling of exile, his desire to belong, is gently anatomized:

> This was never my town,
> I was not born nor bred
> Nor schooled here and she will not
> Have me alive or dead
> But yet she holds my mind
> With her seedy elegance,
> With her gentle veils of rain
> And all her ghosts that walk
> And all that hide behind
> Her Georgian façades—
> The catcalls and the pain,
> The glamour of her squalor,
> The bravado of her talk.

Running through the poem is the attempt to catch the quality of the city's talk, in which he revelled and saw her betray herself. The statues are 'declamatory bronze', the capital's history is in words, 'a fragment of Church latin'; with 'an oratorical phrase' the violence it has seen can be distanced and its lesson forgotten. Irish history reverberates in the European context without that being mentioned, in this and 'Sligo and Mayo' the War is briefly escaped, yet implicit always. MacNeice addresses Dublin in the last stanza:

> You poise the toppling hour—
> O greyness run to flower,
> Grey stone, grey water,
> And brick upon grey brick.

This is taut verse after the appropriate relaxation of *Autumn Journal*, its digressions, extended similes, and metaphors. The last four lines, quoted above, have a beautiful economy: the hour is Europe's, held in slow Ireland whose appropriation of 'all / The alien brought' is an object-lesson in the poise of compromise; the greyness contains both dignity and decay. Mac-Neice's turning of 'run to seed' is an example of the surprising aptness his use of a common phrase does not always achieve; the final line echoes the first, but the circle contains destruction, ruined perfection: 'Nelson on his pillar / Watching his world collapse.'

Stahl and MacNeice proceeded to the north, where the family were staying at the end of Cushendun bay. The house is set down in all its solidity, 'passages of great stone flags / And a walled garden with plums'; nature almost inexplicably persisting in familiar rhythms, itself an unrationed, luxurious commodity, 'the air a glove and water lathering easy'. Blocking all that out is the obsession with radio-listening, 'a little box with a well-bred voice' announcing, as in *Out of the Picture*, the ultimate incongruity.

The last poem of the sequence accepts the fact that 'no one / Can drive the war away' and wonders why the world has not altered to meet it:

> And why, now it has happened,
> And doom all night is lapping at the door,
> Should I remember that I ever met you—
> Once in another world?

Reduced in the *Collected Poems* from ten sections to five, the narrative is sparer, the omission of the love lyrics giving the final poem greater poignancy. These are simple poems, relying on the contrast between natural beauty and human threat, natural indifference and human impotence. Although they concern defeat and offer no way of coping with war and separation except lament, that the poems emerged at all was to MacNeice a positive fact. In 'Broken Windows or Thinking Aloud', an unpublished manuscript dated 1940/41 by Dodds, MacNeice considers the effect of the War on writing. It was probably intended as an article and communicates a sense of exhilarated discovery. For the first time MacNeice comes out directly against the Communist Party, bound to logic whereas he is committed to intuition, and against the pre-War Marxist emphasis on humility: 'we need not be so anxious for self-effacement, we can leave that job to the bombs. This is our time to be arrogant.' He does warn against the denunciation of past selves along with past work, but goes on confidently to distinguish between his thirties' and War poetry:

But different circumstances change the 'message'—the content—and so the method—the style. I notice myself that my two old methods—reportage and lyric—are ceasing to suit me and I notice I have lost my nostalgia, am no longer worried by the passage of time.

Am ready to jettison the past—that is, my personal past. The general and historical Past remains printed in eternity; ...

There are several letters from this period testifying to the same sense of changed direction, or at least to an urge to experiment with different kinds of poetry. The War and the feeling that everything vital to his life had gone into *Autumn Journal* freed him for less self-absorbed writing, and *The Last Ditch* perhaps marks this transition.

The power of MacNeice's poetry in the early 1940s comes from its simplicity: there is less verbal play, fewer arabesques of wit. His lyric gift persists, nostalgia does not. Connolly said that 'he gave the impression of great detachment' (*Radio Portrait*, C. t.), and while this is not a particularly apparent trait in his previous poetry, he now began to develop a distance between himself and the objects he contemplated, was less insistent on the 'I' that saw. Even in 'Meeting Point' Mac-Neice does not identify himself as one of the lovers, nor directly address the woman (as had been his custom in love poems); his not doing so contributes to the sense of almost disembodied enchantment, in which objects exist on new planes of space and time. Each stanza has the same first and last line, enclosing the moment, creating its immobility. Symbols MacNeice had used negatively before—the stopped clock, the desert, music from a radio, a bell—are felicitously transformed. Written before the War, 'Meeting Point' later seemed apt to the period, something snatched from the surrounding destruction which made feeling and sensation preternaturally sharp. The steady poise of the poem, the calm assurance of its repetitions, encapsulate the meeting, providing the only answer to life in time: an art transcending it. And yet the poem is firmly located, two people in a coffee shop, the woman smoking.

> God or whatever means the Good
> Be praised that time can stop like this,
> That what the heart has understood
> Can verify in the body's peace
> God or whatever means the Good.

A similar calm and absence of scepticism informs 'The British Museum Reading Room', written in July 1939. MacNeice is perfectly aware of bogus scholarship, and escapism, and intellectual myopia: 'Some are too much alive and some are asleep, / Hanging like bats in a world of inverted values', but he seems able to afford tolerance. Being walled in by dead words, the nightmare which entered the poems from Iceland and 'Sand in the Air', is now seen as a form of public refuge, a way some hope to 'deaden/ The drumming of the demon in their ears'. Now the fear is palpable, reasonable, domesticating itself in London. MacNeice plants it stealthily amongst the familiar London pigeons, opens briefly an enormous perspective:

> And under the totem poles—the ancient terror—
> Between the enormous fluted Ionic columns
> There seeps from heavily jowled or hawk-like foreign
>   faces
> The guttural sorrow of the refugees.

The other sequence spanning the beginning of the War is 'Novelettes'. While not jettisoning the past, nor demonstrating indifference to the passing of time, MacNeice has shifted his angle.

'The Old Story' (Summer 1939) cannot be a record of Mac-Neice's visit to his ex-wife and her husband in New Jersey, as that took place in October 1940 (he had seen them both in New York in 1939), but the setting seems prophetic. In October they went to Atlantic City, 'which was meant to be a spree but it is hard to have a spree when you are walking with your past'; they promenaded by the grey sea, on grey sand, and afterwards MacNeice sat up late, 'wondering if it made any sense, with Tsalic who had once been a star American footballer and Mariette who had been the best dancer in Oxford'.[8] This direct, bewildered pathos becomes in the poem an act of exorcism, a recognition of emotional deaths. A woman whom he had described in terms of air, light, and especially colour is now as drained of that life as the shore on which they walk: 'With years behind her and waves behind her /Drubbing the memory up and down the pebbles'. MacNeice could scarcely have chosen a more telling verb, with its weight of monotony, harshness, drudgery, but the hurt is given to a third person, narrated not confessed.

The ability to see beyond his own predicament is demonstrated in 'Les Sylphides', the best poem of the group. Part of its success is the result of the tighter control MacNeice exercises over his imagery; in the poems of this period detail is subordinate to a whole. Five of the six stanzas have an appropriate water-image: in the first 'the white sails'; in the second the dancers' naked arms 'moving/ Like seaweed in a pool', suggesting not only their undulant grace but also the ballet's somewhat narcissistic quality; in the third, 'we are floating—ageless, oarless', the stanza which marks the height of romantic, dreamy ecstasy. MacNeice shifts his point of view then to make a general observation, not in the man's tenor, as the dancers depart: 'we cannot continue down / Stream unless we are ready / To enter the lock and drop'. He detaches himself from that choice to drily observe the practical divisions of marriage (compare this with the lines about conjugal loneliness in 'Ec-logue Between the Motherless'), but his compassion goes to the wakeful woman in the final stanza, wondering whether 'It was really worth it and where / The river had flowed away / And where were the white flowers'.

If this were from his personal past, MacNeice was not claiming it as such, and, more surprisingly, he did not elucidate his
connection with 'The Gardener', a portrait of the man who
had been the MacNeices' gardener in Carrickfergus and was
the one link with his mother's time, as his stepmother refused
to employ Roman Catholic servants. Similarly, although the
story of Christina comes directly from his childhood, he dis-
sociates himself from it. In the autobiography, a brief account
of the incident is prefaced by the comment, 'there was always
a sense of loss because things could never be replaced' (p. 37).
The child learns that objects have their separate character:
bricks may be knocked down with impunity and reassembled,
dolls cannot. The grown man discovers nightmare identities.
MacNeice uses regular nursery-rhyme stanzas, where repetition mocks instead of reassuring, enacting the emptiness of
ritual.

> Until the day she tumbled
> And broke herself in two
> And her legs and arms were hollow
> And her yellow head was hollow
> Behind her eyes of blue.

In the prose account, MacNeice takes responsibility for the
breakage, in the poem it is carefully not assigned, fitting the
casualness of 'He went to bed with a lady'.

All the 'Novelettes' involve death in some way, that of love
or of the body, but 'The Preacher' is the most sinister. Graham
Greene's wartime novels feature such landscapes, blitzed and
skeletal: 'old iron, cinders, sizzling dumps / A world castrated,
amputated, trepanned'; the preacher walks in 'the lost acres',
his bedlam vision of humanity taking actual form. The God of
Retribution stalks the poem, the underground world of Greek
myth is present without relief.

By the autumn, MacNeice was writing to Eliot concerning
a projected prose work (*The Strings Are False*), pleased at the
prospect of turning to prose at a time he was producing 'nothing
except short—almost Greek Anthologyish—lyrics' (6 October
1939). A month later he confessed to Dodds that 'the only verse
I am writing now is kind-of-epigrams ...—4 lines going
forward & 4 lines coming back again. I have written about 20

of these.' He added resignedly, 'I expect E. [Eleanor Clark]
would think them awfully "slight".'[9] Indeed, most of them
are; the Greek Anthology character emerges in 'Night Club',
worldly and mordant: 'Salome comes in, bearing / The head of
God knows whom.' The best of the series is the last, 'Didymus',
which is neither personal nor contemporary, although Mac-
Neice uses the image of birds' wings associated previously with
moments of happiness. It was constructed in a manner of
which MacNeice was proud, and he quoted it in a radio discussion with L. A. G. Strong, 'Are There Any Rules?':

> Refusing to fall in love with God, he gave
> Himself to the love of created things,
> Accepting only what he could see, a river
> Full of the shadows of swallows' wings
>
> That dipped and skimmed the water; he would not
> Ask where the water ran or why.
> When he died a swallow seemed to plunge
> Into the reflected, the wrong, sky.

The rules of metre might have dictated a different final line,
but MacNeice wanted to point out both the advantage of fitting
intuition to rules and the scope for breaking them:

I could have written there—'Into the wrong, the reflected sky'—that would
have been a smoother rhythm, but the order of epithets wouldn't have been so
good and quite apart from that, just the sheer sound. I prefer in this poem to
mass the two stresses—'wrong' and 'sky' together. ... That I feel makes you
dwell on the wrongness of it.

In the same debate, he remarked: 'I'm not sure that a pre-
scribed form doesn't often help the poet to clarify his original
impulse', and instancing the Horatian Ode and Villon's Ballade
as examples of useful formal limitation, he mentioned that he
had himself written 'five very regular ballades straight off just
for the interest of it', the previous year.[10]
Drafts for the whole or parts of these are to be found in the
spiral notebook in the Buffalo collection. They are modelled on
Villon's pattern of three eight-line stanzas and an envoy, and
certainly show little hesitation (except for difficulties with the
'Ballade for King Canute'); a stanza might be deleted, but its
replacement is written with only minor changes. Such confidence is also evident in the few poems from *The Earth Compels*

(1938) for which there are drafts; MacNeice appears to be both poetically fertile and technically secure. Two of the ballades were published in American journals and they all appeared in *Poems 1925-1940*, indicating that MacNeice wrote them for a particular audience at that point in the War when he was not involved directly. Perhaps he felt later that they were too much of their time to be preserved.

'Ballade for Mr MacLeish' is the second of the group. It was written before Virginia Woolf's 'Leaning Tower' attack could have been known to MacNeice, but clearly there had been other critics hitting the same nerves. Archibald MacLeish lashed out against the intellectuals in *The Nation* (18 May 1940), labelling them 'The Irresponsibles' because of 'their collective failure to defend "western culture" against the totalitarian threat'.[11] The ballade's opening line is a snide thrust, if MacNeice is addressing rather than including the American poet: 'You say, who read, that we who write / Have failed to do our duty ... '. The refrain, 'You need not tell us what we know', occurs also in an earlier poem 'Men of Good Will' (not collected in any English volume), which admitted that 'our life is slight and ineffectual', that 'we put in words what is topical and transitory'. The ballade is a defensively specious argument, at least in parts. In England in 1940 the *Times Literary Supplement* was asking 'Where are the war poets?': 'The popular press asked the same question, only with patriotic indignation. Soon there were accusations; it was implied that while everyone else had taken up their action stations, the poets had not—and they who had been so noisy about Spain!'[12] This is exactly the kind of hypocrisy against which MacNeice was protesting on a more general front: Day Lewis in his celebrated reply to the clamour caught its irony accurately and with some bitterness. MacNeice asserts that the writers knew the reason for their failure, but he does not elucidate, which is either simple evasion or a refusal to condescend to his opponents' accusatory tactics.

In retrospect, these and the other poems of 1940 look as though they were written in suspension. MacNeice felt at the time that he had found a new direction, an energetic engagement of his being because he was happy in love; he wrote to Dodds with high optimism: '... also I am going to write (at least I hope so) quite new kinds of poems' (from Connecticut, 5 February 1940), and to Mrs Dodds later, with conviction:

Talking about work I am writing a new kind of poetry (very slight so far but will gain body, I hope). ... Am also (this sounds terribly like Wystan too but its all right) formulating a new attitude, the basic principle of which is that Freedom means Getting Into things and not Getting Out of them; also that one must keep making things which are *not oneself*—e.g. works of art, even personal relationships—which must be dry and not damp; as sticking cloves into an orange makes a pomander, = something NEW. (from Ithaca, 22 March 1940)

Yet as the year finished, he was writing his foreword to the Random House *Poems 1925-1940*, and claiming another end and beginning. The tone of the whole is faintly provocative, certainly jaunty: 'When a man collects his poems, people think he is dead. I am collecting mine not because I am dead but because my past life is. Like most other people in the British Isles I have little idea what will happen next. I shall go on writing, but my writing will presumably be different.'

Of course to group the poems of 1940 as poetry of hiatus does not do entire justice to each one, and it should be emphasized that the break between 1939-40 and 1940-1 was not a wrench. Nevertheless what MacNeice called in his letter the quality of dryness, always to some extent present in his work, is as pervasive as the cloves he mentions. It is not the writing of a tourist or a reporter, nor does it stem from the partly confessional impulse that gave rise to *Autumn Journal*. The one intensely personal exception is the sombre and moving 'Autobiography':

> My father made the walls resound,
> He wore his collar the wrong way round.
>
> *Come back early or never come.*
>
> My mother wore a yellow dress;
> Gently, gently, gentleness.
>
> *Come back early or never come.*
>
> When I was five the black dreams came;
> Nothing after was quite the same.
>
> *Come back early or never come.*
>
> The dark was talking to the dead;
> The lamp was dark beside my bed.

There are poems, like this one, of spare form; most are in quatrains, many have very few words to the line. When a poem such as 'Jehu' appears, closer in form to those of the early thirties, it seems clotted and over-insistent: reaching for symbols of what the War might be, it has little imaginative power set beside the poems MacNeice wrote back in London, having undergone the Blitz. The experience of being, as he wrote to Dodds, 'timelessly happy', perhaps accounts for the persistent optimism of the poems' endings: however melancholy their burden, there is nearly always hope and expansion in the last lines. The poem does not circumscribe the experience, but launches it.

Two poems from the period for which drafts are extant prove exceptions to this generalization. 'Stylite' and 'Entirely' were written in March 1940, a prolific month for MacNeice. For 'Stylite' there are three attempts at the second stanza: on facing pages the poem stands nearly in its printed form (Buffalo: spiral notebook). The notebook gives no clue as to how the poem occurred to MacNeice, or from whence sprang the god on the other pillar. It is mysterious and austere; it personifies the opposition of Christian and Hellenic culture. The petrified (literally, though MacNeice often attaches the word figuratively to the Church) saint, with his consciousness of guilt and his determination to exclude the world, at the moment of instinctive reaction—in the face of death—has to recognize physical beauty, sensuality, and worldliness in the form of 'A white Greek god, / ... his eyes on the world'.

A similar sense of the poem's being 'given' is found in 'Entirely': on one page of the spiral notebook its first two stanzas are jotted down in pencil, with few alterations; two pages later the whole poem is inked between the address of the *Southern Review* and some doodles, in the form in which it was published. The apparent effortlessness of its composition suits the airiness of the work itself. Such changes as were made foster ease:

> And when we try to eavesdrop on the *great*
>   Presences it is rarely
> That *by a stroke of luck we can* appropriate
>   Even a phrase entirely. (my italics)

The object of eavesdrop began as 'the gods', then 'the dark', before MacNeice settled on his more neutral and flexible 'great presences'; while the pedestrian 'we can catch and then appropriate' underwent a blithe substitution. In stanza two, 'Bell or siren banishes the blue / *Eyes of Love* entirely', the vivid physical image was originally merely 'anyone else': perhaps MacNeice looked back a few pages to a deleted poem on the human obsession with happiness, which included the lines 'But the bony body / & the blue eye / Of Nature ... ', and rescued the lines for a new context. The bell as destroyer of joy is a recurrent image, probably attributable to childhood associations, but here it does not dislodge potential. Despite the poem's insistence on the frustrations of experience, the buoyancy of its rhythm, the frequency of run-on lines, and the swift succession of images give it an ironic optimism. It encompasses both the delicacy of 'All we know is the splash of words in passing / And falling twigs of song', and the turbulent 'mad weir of tigerish waters'. 'Entirely' is the most attractive and persuasive statement Mac-Neice made of his inability to be dogmatic—in art or love or the world—though that was not, presumably, the poem's purpose.

The old themes of exile, home, and journeying continue in this period, appropriately. They have direct relevance to the hundreds of war-created refugees, whom MacNeice considers in his poem of that name, 'disintered from Europe' and arriving in New York, with modest enough hopes and all the mystery of the continent before them. It is one of the poems that eventually opens on to dizzying prospects: '... they still feel / The movement of the ship while through their imagination / The known and unheard-of constellations wheel'. There is the long catalogue 'The Sense of Smell' (which only appeared in *Poems 1925-1940*), unadulterated and sensuous nostalgia: 'Turf-smoke for Ireland', 'French fern soap / And bath powder'; evoking 'a vanished/April, an ended / Voyage, a picnic ...'; listing 'How many delights? / How many adieus?'; too self-indulgent to be retained. This search for lost worlds, from the distance living in America provided, takes some of its impetus from dreams: one briefly encountered in 'Eclogue from Iceland'—the B text—is expanded in 'Order to View'; the bleak house and mouldering garden,

> The bell-pull would not pull
> And the whole place, one might
> Have supposed, was deadly ill:
> The world was closed,

which are transformed by a tree shaken by the wind, a movement of clouds:

> Somewhere in a loose-box
> A horse neighed
> And all the curtains flew out of
> The windows; the world was open.

The extreme suggestiveness of the poem lies in the metaphors
being so simple and capable of containing a spectrum of interpretation: home-coming, reconciliation, *déjà vu*, rejuvenation,
the random nature of illumination, the surprise and excitement
of its occurrence, of the form it takes. It may even be an image
of derelict England. In 'Experience with Images' MacNeice
links this with 'The Dowser', which also ends in unexpected
discovery, as poems 'which are a blend of rational allegory and
dream suggestiveness'.

  Both the Random House collection and *Plant and Phantom*
close with the 'Cradle Song for Eleanor'. Twelve years before,
MacNeice had written a 'Cradle Song for Miriam', which was
really an excuse for playing with metaphors of muddle and
confusion, calling on a bored deity, and paying very little
attention to Miriam (Mary?). Whereas in 1928 a reader might
have sensed his wanting attention himself, imposing a theory
of the universe on the poem, in 1940 MacNeice is a spectator
still but actually knows what he sees, knows the precariousness
of his disengagement. Eleanor he asks to

> Sleep and, asleep, forget
>   The watchers on the wall
> Awake all night who know
>   The pity of it all.

Impersonal meditations emerge from the post-American
period too, but there are many poems in which MacNeice tries
on other voices, other habits. Writing about Keats's description
of the poetical character, he commented: 'That a poet has no
identity is a useful half-truth, for it counteracts the common

opinion that a poet is some one hawking his own personality.'[13] The War forced him to be engaged in the community, which may have fostered an ability to identify with different lives. It also saw the second phase of MacNeice's obsession with death and loss: that moves out of the personal sphere and the disguises of nightmare, because the threats were imminent and tangible, oddly stimulating. In 'Broken Windows' there is the relief of attack, finally, after the years of private and public vacillation:

And why not shelve your private salvation and see what you can do with the world? Without bothering too much about life—your own—or life with a capital L, and taking special care not to think of death as cancellation ...

Death in its own right—as War does incidentally—sets our lives in perspective. ... Death as a leveller also unites us in life and Death not only levels but differentiates—it crystallises our deeds.

... But applied science, by shattering a town overnight, by superimposing upon ordered decay a fantastic but palpable madness, has shown us the integral function of death. Death is the opposite of decay; a stimulus, a necessary horizon.

The world at war, however, imposed its tasks and did not leave a great deal of room for individual manoeuvre. MacNeice found in the atmosphere of threatened London exactly that sense of community whose passing from more primitive regions he had regretted, but he also feared that the necessity for collective effort, for accepting the dictates of Authority, would encourage a uniformity and lack of initiative which might persist after the War. So while he celebrated the one, he campaigned against the other, as in his article 'The Way We Live Now' for *Penguin New Writing* (April 1941). Still holding to his Irishness, and indeed to his preference for America as a place in which to live and write, MacNeice was nevertheless glad to be in London. Since the Blitz it had 'become more comprehensible. Because this great dirty, slovenly, sprawling city is a visible and tangible symbol of freedom'.

In 1941 MacNeice published as much prose as poetry: he reviewed films for the *Spectator*, books for the *New Statesman*, recorded some American impressions for *Horizon* (which had come into existence in January 1940), and for five months wrote a 'London Letter' for the American journal *Common Sense*. Most of the letters are quasi-political and fairly critical of the government's handling of the Home Front: '... the Ministry of Food is still too timid to organise (it hardly even co-operates with the Ministry of Agriculture)' (June 1941, p. 175); and he kept a vigilant eye on any suppression of free speech. The letters admit to mess and muddle, yet are convinced that attitudes are changing, positive things emerging. The best of them is an account of the April raids, one of which had become known as 'the Wednesday', and 'the Saturday' raid in May which hit the House of Commons, and was to be the last major German bombing effort. On 10 May MacNeice was fire-watching from St. Paul's: 'great tawny clouds of smoke, rolling in a sumptuous Baroque exuberance, had hidden the river completely and there we were on the dome, a classical island in a more than Romantic Inferno'. He wrote that it was astonishing and absolutely impossible to describe, the old clichés 'are utterly and insultingly inadequate' (July 1941, p. 206).

Nevertheless he attempted to do it in poetry, as did Day Lewis and Dylan Thomas. His prose description reaches for the exact shades of flame, the surrealist combination of objects glimpsed in roofless, half-walled buildings, and for the layers of feeling the fires prompted: exhilaration, awe, fear, sadness. The poems are not concerned with appearance—as they probably would have been ten years earlier—so much as with the complex reaction of mind and heart to these events. MacNeice found a way to cope with their incredibility by making them a part of a Grimm fantasy. He asserts against the lumbering, mindless destruction the nimbleness of the maker, quick-footed and triumphant words: '... The trolls can occasion / Our death but they are not able / To use it as we can use it.' While 'The Trolls' after a masterly first section becomes repetitive in its insistence on man's capacity to survive 'the crawl of lava', in 'Troll's Courtship' the slight clumsiness is exactly appropriate to the lonely troll going to immense trouble over futile display. The idea that the raids are an attempt to woo by destruction hints at the truth MacNeice articulated in 'Brother Fire' the next year:

> O delicate walker, babbler, dialectician Fire,
> O enemy and image of ourselves,
> Did we not on those mornings after the All Clear,

> When you were looting shops in elemental joy
> And singing as you swarmed up city block and spire,
> Echo your thought in ours? 'Destroy! Destroy!'[14]

MacNeice's job amongst all this was officially to provide the
words that would make war experiences comprehensible to
those not undergoing them: broadcasts about damaged buildings in London, for instance, for an American audience, and
later programmes about Russia, Yugoslavia, and Greece for
home consumption. Propagandizing despite his earlier distaste
for the task, and associating with a frequently dispirited intelligentsia, MacNeice expended not a little of his poetic energy
worrying at the efficacy of verbal communication. Robert
Hewison, in his account of London's literary life *Under Siege*,
maps out the territory haunted by the writers during the War,
Fitzrovia and Soho, and quotes MacNeice when talking about
the stimulus and drawbacks of the pub world, the 'factitious
popular front in booze' which he mocks in 'Alcohol':

> Take away your slogans; give us something to
>   swallow,
> Give us beer or brandy or schnapps or gin;
> This is the only road for the self-betrayed to follow—
> The last way out that leads not out but in.

The notion that, however distant from physical action, each
man took some responsibility for the havoc of war, is linked in
the poems with religious images. When MacNeice used the
Bible or Christianity in his earlier work, it was usually in a
needling or satirical fashion, as one very familiar but uncom-
fortable with them, sometimes outright defiant. His more
tolerant, genuinely puzzled, and inquiring attitude in the forties
is that of a man who has grown past the need to repudiate his
family's ethos, and—though in no simple sense—has been
forced by war to re-examination. He concluded the Blitz letter
to America, his last one, with a kind of manifesto:

... sometimes I say to myself 'This is mere chaos, it makes no sense,' and at
other times I think 'Before I saw war-time London I must have been spiritually colour-blind' ... There is, in some quarters, an understandable swing-
back to religion but the revival of religion (with its ordinary connotations) is
something I neither expect nor desire. What *is* being forced upon people is
a revival of the religious sense. And after the hand-to-mouth ethics of 19th

century liberalism and the inverted and blinkered quasi-religion of Marxism and the sentimentality of the Lost Generation—after all that, we need all the senses we were born with; and one of those is the religious.

This was an old battleground for him and perhaps always remained a source of sadness, that he could neither accept his father's faith nor be content with the hiatus its absence left. To endorse a system would have been to falsify his belief in the world's being 'incorrigibly plural'; Dodds felt that his ambiguous attitude towards religion came from the conflict between fascination for imaginative constructs and empirical common sense. Some transcendent sense persisted, yet Mac-Neice was trapped by it; not having a basis of genuine mystical conviction, his poems could tip over into sentimentality, as in *The Kingdom*. The recurrent use of Christian imagery seems to indicate that it corresponded to some level of his experience, like the organic pattern of meaning discerned in 'The Newsreel', to be surrendered to almost ignorantly: 'Something half-conjectured and half-divined'.

Where religious symbols or a search for a pattern might be expected, neither is to be found. In *Autumn Sequel* (1954) Mac-Neice gives a circumstantial account of his hearing the news of Graham Shepard's death ('Gavin' in the poem); in two previous poems he had spelt out what that loss meant. Perhaps it was this and his father's decease that sent MacNeice back to the past he thought he had jettisoned; it certainly reasserts itself in *Holes in the Sky* (1948). 'The Casualty (in memorium G.H.S.)' appears in *Springboard* (1944).

To the Spring 1941 edition of *Folios of New Writing*, MacNeice contributed a poem which has understandably not been reprinted, titled 'Casualty of War (New York)'. It is in an odd form, couplets interspersed with free verse, and turns upon the time difference between England and America, a part of the distance between the living and the dead. The poet is unengaged in the event he describes, he lines up what seem to be appropriate metaphors for death, but they do not touch emotional reality. He is not entirely at ease when writing of Shepard's death either: grief may have been, for MacNeice, an uncommunicable emotion.

There are two versions of 'The Casualty' in the Texas collection. One, possibly a first draft, is to be found in a BBC

notebook, and can be dated *c*.October 1943. The other is a
four-page autograph manuscript, with some emendations. At
a late stage the poem was prefaced by a line from Dante,
'Lascio lo fele e vo per dolci pomi', which is consolatory, but
MacNeice may have felt it too literary and out of character with
the opening, or decided that it did not match the poem's concentration on his friends' loss rather than Shepard's fate.[15] The
title deleted from the manuscript, 'One out of many', was
better abandoned for the chosen title, which conveys the fact
that Shepard was simply a casualty of war along with all the
others, but also the one whose dying most touched MacNeice.

The notebook draft reveals that he had some trouble in
writing the poem: there was the natural emotional difficulty
complicated by awareness of literary antecedents in the elegy,
especially for death by water. The combination of loving praise
and the inconceivable voyage to the centre, of jauntiness and
gravity, does not quite come off. The colloquial opening, with
the force of the living personality still felt to be undiminished,
could be combined with an evocation of Homer, but the transition between the two is uncomfortably reminiscent of the
Cheshire Cat: '... and you would grin / Dwindling to where the
fading star allures'. When the poem has to consider the actual
means of death (Shepard's corvette was torpedoed), MacNeice
handles it much better, the break between the second and third
stanzas enacting his point: '... they will not sever // That thread
of so articulate silence'.

He sees the death as another of the experiences they might
have talked over, yet void where there might have been an
answer. In the sixth stanza MacNeice had written in the notebook:

> How was it then? How is it? You & I
> Have often since we were children discussed death
> & giggled at the preachers and wondered how
> They cd talk so big about mortality
> & immortality more. But you yourself cd now
> Talk big as any—if you had the breath.

This he altered only slightly; in the page draft 'giggled' became
'sniggered'. The former implies simply finding such talk funny,
if embarrassing; the latter is more knowing, mocking, and

makes a better transition to the dead Shepard, encompassing
both the shallowness of their reaction then and MacNeice's
existing ignorance. At first he addresses his friend in the tense
of continuance, then switches to the past; the closing qualification recalls 'In Memory of Major Robert Gregory'—'I am
accustomed to their lack of breath'—though MacNeice's uneasy control of tone does not compare with Yeats's muscular
grace. Writing about Yeats's treatment of his friends in poetry,
MacNeice likened it to Shakespeare's: '... the hero is conceded
full individuality, his Marxist conditioning is ignored. This
means simplification ... the explanation of a man not by his
daily life but by one or two great moments' (*Yeats*, p. 110). He
himself worked in the opposite way: while death provided a
singular and unifying perspective, against it MacNeice hurled
every disparate memory he could catch, a riot of snapshots
attesting to movement and confusion, to dailiness. At the same
time, as Yeats's concern was to present Gregory as one of a
Renaissance company, so MacNeice wanted to claim for
Shepard more than potential. His sociable life, with his perception of folly as well as delight in geniality, was complemented
by an inhabitance of the world 'beyond the spiked / Railing
where in the night some old blind minstrel begs'. MacNeice
had written 'the blinded minstrel': he eventually changed it
probably because it too clearly anticipated the identification he
went on to make. In the notebook draft the claim at first was
modest: 'He begged & you responded, being yourself / One of
his kind', but was immediately enlarged to: 'Like Raftery or
Homer, one of his kind—'.

MacNeice then twice seeks to convey the contrast of this
many-faceted existence with its ending: 'your multi-coloured
passion / Having been merged by death in universal Blue',
reads lamely like an advertisement; 'O did you / Make one last
integration, find a Form / Grow out of formlessness when the
Atlantic hid you?' The abstraction has dignity; MacNeice's
tone is not of facetious curiosity but of longing for reassurance;
the rhyme carries the poem's burden of a finality that is yet un-
accepted.

The long stretch of fluency MacNeice enjoyed had ended in
about 1943, one of its late products being the song-cycle he

wrote for Hedli Anderson, unpublished—except for one lyric—until 1975. Taking a dislike to the Giraud/Schönberg *Pierrot Lunaire* she was performing before their marriage, he casually announced his intention to compose for her, and 'equally casually ... he sat down and wrote [*The Revenant*]'.[16] The cycle of twelve songs and eleven interludes is simply worded, reliant on repetition and rhyme, and on alliterative balance in the interludes. It reads as though it has been tossed off, a charming gift.

The poems of the mid- to late 1940s are more laboured over. Some of them are emended with a ballpoint pen—they are almost always composed in pencil—which suggests that they were not written at one sitting, as appears to have been the case with earlier poems. The exigencies of wartime composition, or pressure of work, may have helped to modify MacNeice's habits. Careful revision is particularly noticeable in the poems for *Holes in the Sky*: the eight lines of 'Corner Seat', for example, went through four versions, their final form being reached in an alteration of the galley proofs. The process made it tighter, adjectives were cut (drafts at Berg and Texas). The plainer statements of the printed poem make its hollowness more apparent: the images of windows, reflections, and trains are so characteristic of MacNeice. His revisions did not always simplify; another train poem in the volume, 'Slow Movement', becomes increasingly complex (Texas).

Holes in the Sky, MacNeice's fourth collection in the decade, is the last to be dominated by the War and reckons with the strangeness of that ending, the reassertion of things forced underground: 'The kings who slept in the caves are awake and out' ('The National Gallery'). There is the brilliant Blitz ballad 'The Streets of Laredo', then all the poems, puzzled in varying degrees, which register the cessation of bombing, fighting, and black-outs. The thirties' schoolboys are now men,

> Having kept vigil on the Unholy Mount
> And found some dark and tentative things made clear,
> Some clear made dark, in the years that did not
>   count.

> ('Hiatus')

Separated couples are reunited, uncertainly: 'For all green Nature has gone out of gear / Since they were apart and

hoping, since last year' ('Bluebells'). The death of friends
mocks at the world reforming: 'That the world will never be
quite—what a cliché—the same again ...'; this poem, 'Tam
Cari Capitis', obviously harks back to the elegy for Shepard,
taking its title from Horace's *Odes*, I.24, the line MacNeice
translated, 'Why moderate our grief for one so dear?' In the
same month, July 1946, he wrote 'The Cyclist', drawing on the
memory of a ride out from Marlborough with Shepard, when
'all the white horses were wishes' (*Strings*, p. 88). Like 'The
Casualty' it is concerned with stasis, but here of joy, of sensuous
integration (in 'Street Scene' art can provide such a moment,
when the crippled singer 'Hitting her top note holds our own
lame hours in equipoise'); the boy riding the hill and the heat,
before hitting the valley:

> For ten seconds more can move as the horse in the
>   chalk
> Moves unbeginningly calmly
> Calmly regardless of tenses and final clauses
> Calmly unendingly moves.

MacNeice wrote to Dodds from Achill at the end of July
1945, 'During the last two months I have written eleven poems
(after a year long lull).' *Holes in the Sky* reveals an altered approach, the poems being generally less concentrated than in the
preceding three collections, and frequently reverting to his
personal past. This was no doubt given impetus by a long stay
in Ireland, and a renewed connection with the country was
marked by MacNeice's appointment as Poetry Editor for the
flourishing Irish periodical *The Bell*, to which he contributed
poems in 1946. As he writes in 'Carrick Revisited', 'Memories
I had shelved peer at me from the shelf.'

   The astonishment voiced in this poem bridges gulfs: between
childhood and adulthood, one war and another, catching the
surprise of attachment to that from which so much subsequent
experience had alienated him. From his return to 'the Norman
bridgehead ... the garrison town' (as he wrote in a cancelled
draft for stanza five; Texas), MacNeice abstracts the significance of any locality for any person:

> Time and place—our bridgeheads into reality
> But also its concealment! Out of the sea

We land on the Particular and lose
All other possible bird's-eye views, the Truth
That is of Itself for Itself—but not for me.

It is an admission that he cannot utter a final valediction, as he
had once attempted; at the same time as acknowledging his
'childhood's frame' to be inescapable, he does not extend any
affection to Carrickfergus. Each stanza ends on the note of
something awry: the resignation that it should be so is tinged,
still, with disbelief.

MacNeice retraces steps too in 'The Strand', in its reticence
praising his father more than the direct eulogy to be found in
The Kingdom. He hints at the complexities of his relationship
with his father, and the metaphysical reaches of their skirmishes,
without going beyond the simple familiarity of the scene he
sets. The apparent ease with which he handles the *terza rima*
form was perhaps his first indication that he could use it at
much greater length, although not, it may be thought, to such
advantage. His association of natural phenomena with their
portrayal in art ('White Tintoretto clouds'), especially with the
dramatic Venetian painter, sets him apart from someone
'Carrying his boots and paddling like a child'—the sensuous
quality of 'my naked feet' on the wet sand is quite absent—while
MacNeice also repeats his father's steps; like the mirrored
clouds, is this a true or illusory repetition? He has already
judged that mirror, it only 'imputes a lasting mood / To island
truancies'. Like his parent he is escaping from duty or routine:
there is the faint suggestion that a boy, having seen his father
unbend so far, might have thought the mood would linger back
in the ordinary world. The clerical 'black figure whom the
horizon understood' is belatedly identified, and the assessment
is that of an adult son, it attests to his perception of the man's
relation with the infinite. MacNeice catches the childlike
quality, the devotion, the element of something 'solitary and
wild' in his father, and also the strength that enabled him among
other things to take his unpopular political stand; this he
transfers to the landscape, but it is the Bishop who is 'Eyeing
the flange of steel in the turning belt of brine'. Father and son
are linked by the same experience, whose meaning for the
former we might guess at; for the latter, uncertainty prevails.
Ending as he does with a notation of natural fact, and the

departure of visitors for home, MacNeice encompasses both his
own continuing life and his father's death, since images of sea,
shore, and of home are familiar to those accustomed to Anglican
prayers as metaphors for the soul's passage and arrival.

A month before writing 'The Strand' MacNeice had already
been occupied with the theme of the contrast between his
English and his Irish life, and its personification in himself and
his father:

> Thus from a city when my father would frame
> Escape, he thought, as I do, of bog or rock
> But I have also this other, this English, choice
> Into what yet is foreign; whatever its name
> Each wood is the mystery and the recurring shock
> Of its dark coolness is a foreign voice.
>
> ('Woods')

MacNeice deliberately opposes his view of woods, coloured by
art, to his father's reaction, 'who found the English landscape
tame'. He concedes that their proximity to villages emphasizes
their limits, that emerging from the woods one finds 'an ordered
open air long ruled by dyke and fence':

> They are not like the wilds of Mayo, they are assured
> Of their place by men; reprieved from the neolithic
>   night
> By gamekeepers or by Herrick's girls at play.

This association with literature, and the more powerful glamour
cast on the woods by the boy's reading of Malory and fairy-
tales, is the recreation of imaginative truth that had been
bypassed in the War's urgency, or transmuted—as in the troll
poems—into harshness. It reappears too in 'Autolycus', where
MacNeice celebrates Shakespeare's ability to conjure the en-
chanted world. The poem ends with MacNeice's assertion of
their common bond, the chaotic environment in which each
found himself; his more convincing tribute goes to the minor
poets.

The compression which the *TLS* reviewer found generally
wanting in *Holes in the Sky* is not proper to the subject of 'Elegy
for Minor Poets', 'Who often found their way to pleasant
meadows'. Texas holds three versions of the poem: a draft with

heavy revisions, perhaps the first; an autograph manuscript with some emendations, and a pencilled fair copy. The tone of the poem is set by the first alteration. MacNeice began it, 'Who frequently attained to ...', and by his substitution conveyed the chanciness of their discoveries, lands leisurely encountered, not driven towards. This hesitancy of purpose is underlined by his changing in the second stanza 'they *handled* the same language' to 'fingered'.

The first Texas version continues with what is printed as stanza four, followed by the present stanza three, then the present sixth stanza, the fifth being written out on another page without alterations. MacNeice was certain of his first line, 'And give the benefit of the doubtful summer', and of the last, but the development of the poets' missed opportunities in fitting terms caused him some trouble, and his indulgence to them he eventually extended to himself over one phrase.

worshipped the
To those who ~~stayed indoors~~ sky but stayed indoors
Chained to a [~~clerical~~] desk or ~~prevented by the spirit's~~
~~Hayfever inhibitions prevented by material needs or the~~
by duty
some mental
From by ~~social duty circumstances~~ or by ~~the spirit's~~
~~Ironical~~ Hayfever. Across those office or study floors
on to
Let the sun ~~creep &~~ clamber ~~up on their~~ open ~~notebooks~~
shine
& fill in what they groped for between each line.

In the lightly emended manuscript, the third line stands as:
conscience
'Bound to a desk by ~~duties~~   or ~~by a mental~~ ~~intellectual~~ /
Hayfever'. It eventually reverts to the original 'spirit's hay-fever', which is slick rather than thoughtful.

Perhaps MacNeice added what is now the third stanza recalling *Enemies of Promise*, in which he was cited among his literary contemporaries as a cautionary example: drink, sex, and domesticity were some of the obstacles to writing Connolly had labelled. The stanza's mention of great talkers touches on MacNeice's Irish inheritance, and on his contention that poetry

is a natural extension of conversation: 'Who were the world's
Inspired
best talkers, their intonations / ~~Exact~~ but as writers ~~lost~~ lacked
that sense of touch'. 'Superb' was written in the margin to
replace the proposed adjectives; the later change to 'in tone and
rhythm / Superb' gives their talk more body.

After relegating these minor ones to their place in the estab-
lishment, at least mimicking the tone in which they are assigned
their various functions, but dissociating himself from it ('Some
of their names—not all—we learnt in school'), MacNeice closes
the elegy in praise, making common his and their cause. There
is charity in this, not the grudging community he allows with
Shakespeare in the next poem ('though more self-reliant /
Than we, you too were born and grew up in a fix'). Still,
settling on the precise nature of this shared endeavour was not
easy:

who, unlike them, stay young
In spite of—partly because of— ~~which, we later~~

~~shd underwrite~~
~~their debts~~

~~inheritors of their debts~~
Suitors to their mistress, ~~gamblers with their dice~~
Shd hang the graves of each   a flower or medal
with
~~Shd raise them each his trophy~~   his appropriate trophy
Such as each might have wished to find there hung
on
Do right to hang the grave of each ~~with~~ a trophy
had he been solvent
~~ed he have paid for it,~~ he might himself have
Such as ~~he or we~~ (though might choose to have hung
~~a In a forgotten field~~

~~that~~
Above ~~an forgetful~~ forgetfulness   ~~forgets its ancient corn~~

~~We underwrote his debts before we were born~~
surmount
Above themselves: these gamblers ~~are above~~ our scorn
~~These gamblers graves we should not, must not scorn~~
had underwritten)
Whose debts we underwrote   ) before we were born.

The concept of indebtedness was there almost from the start:
for the gravity of the stanza MacNeice pruned away the natural
images, choosing to emphasize the formality of the transaction
between generations of the minor poets. It is a graceful main-
tenance of his old line about poetry, and lends a touch of
grandeur to the least literary undertaking: '... these debtors
preclude our scorn— / Did we not underwrite them when we
were born?' We might see it as a sign of poetic re-establishment,
of MacNeice's linking himself to a tradition—however loosely
conceived—that matches his return to themes temporarily
eclipsed by the War. But he is, in the mid-forties, a somewhat
wearied suitor 'to their mistress'.

IV. THE MIDDLE STRETCH

The 'necessary horizon' provided by death now began to recede, and although the release from tension was vital to his general well-being, it was not advantageous to MacNeice's poetry. Relaxation into much longer poems testified to a regained sense of stability, but the more he shows signs of being driven, by powerful emotion or by external events—as in *Autumn Journal*—, the more rewarding is his work. Then the dialectic is between an initiating force and the controlling imagination, a tension lost when domination is too easy or when solutions are imposed. MacNeice's fluency was seductive and this period finds him tending to succumb. On reading *Springboard*, Auden wrote commending 'Prayer Before Birth' above everything ('Troll's Courtship' was one of his favourites); he suspected MacNeice to be

an 'anima naturaliter Christiana', which means that when you try to be a Classical Humanist, as in some passages in *The Kingdom*, I imagine I detect a certain lack of conviction. I'm glad you're moving away from the elegant detail, 'the triple mirror' etc to a more chastened and abstract style, not because you don't handle the former beautifully and better than any of us, but just because you can do that standing on your head. (21 January 1945)

The Kingdom was the longest poem of the war years; it celebrated not that possibility of concerted action MacNeice canvassed in *Autumn Journal*, praised in his wartime articles, and was required to salute in broadcasts, but the sheer existence of 'the Kingdom of individuals'. He appended a note to *Springboard* concerning the use of the definite article in many titles for the volume: he was not offering 'a set of Theophrastean characters. "The Conscript" does not stand for all conscripts but an imagined individual; any such individual seems to me to have an absolute quality which the definite article recognises.' Yet this quality certainly resembles that essence of character which a moralist tries to pin down. In poems such as 'The Libertine' or 'The Mixer', desolation gives the portrayal its edge, whereas the unexpected idealization of the cast of *The Kingdom* muzzles MacNeice's power, reducing some lines to caricature.

It is commonly said of MacNeice that the BBC took its toll, in terms of time and diversion of his talent. Writing for radio in

fact had a discernible influence on his poetry (*The Kingdom* being
an apt illustration), encouraging a manner he had to learn to
discard. If we set aside the dramatic successes such as *The Dark
Tower*, and the anthology programmes involving a choice of
other poets' work, the remainder may be said to rely on the
technique of the representative voice. A feature programme
required the swift and intelligent assimilation of a great deal of
factual information, and a sense of the appropriate landscape
or atmosphere. MacNeice's general method was to attack his
subject through a collection of voices that could counterpoint
impressions and offer facts relevant to their perspective. In a
programme on Delhi he used a nanny and a missionary, among
others (*Portrait of Delhi*, 2 May 1948); in *India at First Sight*
(13 March 1948) he gave voices to History, Topography,
Literature, and Ignorance; to characterize Vienna, interp-
olations from Mozart, Beethoven, 'lieber Augustin', Hitler
(*Vienna*, 12 March 1942). Thus he became accustomed to cutting
from one voice to another, each with its distinguishing trick of
style, and also to vignettes of character or landscape features.
It made interesting listening; it must also have reinforced
tendencies towards superficiality and concentration on detail,
not the abstraction for which Auden had hoped. Valentin
Iremonger, in a review of *The Dark Tower and Other Radio Scripts*,
made the trenchant criticism that radio would affect MacNeice's
work because of its 'depreciating for the poet the value of individual words'; what counted was the dramatic buildup.[1] His
broadcasting colleagues have attested to MacNeice's acute
sense of the potential of a script and his ability to make it
effective: William Empson said of the War period that 'Louis
was a tower of strength for putting on little elegant features
about boating on the lakes of Nanking or what not' (*Radio
Portrait*, C.t.). The craftsman's approach was typical of Mac-
Neice and he appreciated radio's demands; that they might
not have served his poetry well, he never publicly acknowledged.
It should be remembered too that during the War, when he
wrote his greatest number of scripts, he was also poetically
prolific, composing some of his best poems.

Although three of the characters in *The Kingdom* are specifically
British—the old man 'dressed in tweeds like a squire' (probably
a portrait of his Sherborne headmaster, Littleton Powys), 'Our

Mother' in section III, and the dead man in section VII (Bishop MacNeice)—the pressure of international events has shaped their portrayal. MacNeice's broadcasts were concerned with allied efforts to resist Germany, for example the mobilization of entire cities like Leningrad, and underground activities in Greece and Yugoslavia. Despite the necessary simplicity of their message, these programmes were not the kind of propaganda of which MacNeice might be ashamed. He saluted human qualities beyond nationality: patience, courage, self-sacrifice, integrity, steadfastness, faith. Having to present national pride and endeavour, he did so through individuals with whom listeners could identify. *The Kingdom* also has this dual emphasis, on distinctiveness and on cohesion. As in the broadcasts MacNeice had no political solution to offer beyond the devotion to freedom, so in the poem he does not specify the belief by which his characters live (except in section VII); their salvation need not be religious, their motivation may not even be consciously articulated. A refusal to be dogmatic can be a personal strength, and in this area it is obvious why MacNeice did not wish to proselytize, yet it is not always valuable for poetry. Auden mentions a lack of conviction; there is also a diffuseness, an inclusiveness that is generous but lacks rigour. It was an effort to go beyond the poses rejected at the end of *Autumn Journal* and beyond the various facile political solutions to the problem of preserving both individuality and community, or the exigent answers provided by the War. For all Mac-Neice's skill and care, it does not ring true.

Nevertheless, the poem indicated the contemplative turn his work was to take in this difficult period. It fitted in with the direction he saw as generally profitable for British writing, which he discussed in two articles proposed for *The New York Times*, in July and August 1945. MacNeice remarked on the change from the 'facile internationalism' of the pre-war years to the new isolation of the War, which was also fertilized by contact with *émigré* European intellectuals; from the 'chunk-of-life realism' to an intensified religious note in poetry. He maintained that although there had been relatively little direct description of horror and violence, the War would be fermenting in writers' imaginations: 'the good writer will still be the better for having a journalist inside him'. The second article is partly a denunciation of the wholesale swallowing of dogma; Mac-Neice stated that writers had 'regained both humility and dignity. ... We are turning away from the kind of specialisation which means a mutilation of the world.' In prose he saw signs of a possible 'fusion of symbolism and realism', a return to attention to form. His poetic predictions were optimistic. The thirties' poets had weathered better than prose writers he thought; the War had caused them to grow out of 'their more childish disabilities' and had closed the gap on either side. They were closer to Eliot because of a 'renewed religious sense—or, at the least, a wider gamut of values', and to the younger generation, whose 'dangerous youth has made them both humane and mystical'.[2] He concluded that their values, 'as is consonant with Britain's position in the world', would henceforward be 'qualitative rather than quantitative, i.e. spiritual rather than material'.

Geoffrey Grigson diverged very sharply from these opinions when he diagnosed the state of British poetry in 1949 and looked back on his own hopes for it in the thirties. In his introduction to *Poetry of the Present*, he recorded his initial repulsion from MacNeice's early poetry, 'a little mixed perhaps with the effect of the dark undergraduate stalking ... in a cloak about the deep lanes of Oxford', and then his growing respect for it: 'The icicles, the ice-cream, the pink and white, the lace and the froth and the fireworks were still there, but underneath the game was the drop, the space and the knowledge.' With Eliot as stimulant, and Auden and MacNeice widening the territory open to poets, Grigson had felt secure in stating—in a foreword to a selection of poems from *New Verse*—that a common-sense view of poetry was the only one acceptable, and that 'if a poem (or a mind) is more than the sum of its details and constituents, that extra something is explicable in material terms'. Naturally the neo-Romantic upsurge had disappointed him, in fact he described it in terms of a recurrence of disease, and complained that there had been 'a weakening then of the penicillin in which one had trusted'. Loyal to the poets whom he had published, Grigson did not indulge in more direct criticism than that. His final generalization, however, was damning:

The First War shocked several writers and painters into a sudden humanity devoid of sham, and left a few of them changed and receptive. The Second

War shocked other writers and painters out of themselves or out of healthier modes into mystifyings or commonplaces moribundly imaged and dressed. One war killed much sham; the other revived it, as a refuge, at least in frail and noisy talents.[3]

Presumably the last qualification exempts MacNeice from these strictures.

The poems MacNeice wrote after the War often suffer from a sense of being steered to a predetermined course, and as they lengthen they lose impetus. Eliot rehearsed the necessity for dull patches in long poems, which MacNeice endorsed in 'Experiences with Images' (p. 132), but Eliot's practice in the *Four Quartets* was to wrestle with problems of expression openly, to enact his difficulties as part of the poem's strategy. Mac-Neice, on the other hand, manages to push a poem ahead without its really developing: in *The Stygian Banks* he takes seven sections to elaborate a theme which could have been comfortably contained in one. The title is apter than intended, in that the poem lingers between two worlds, neither sufficiently realized.

MacNeice gave a clue to his intentions when he remarked: 'The same quasi-musical interlinking of images, with variations on contrasted themes, is used ... with a more leisurely cumulative effect, in a recent long poem, *The Stygian Banks*. Such poems are tentative, though unforced, essays in the genre in which Rilke achieved such astonishing exactitude' ('Images', p. 132). He would have read Leishman's translations of Rilke, published at intervals throughout the thirties; Spender collaborated with Leishman on a translation of the *Duino Elegies* published in 1939 (a version by Victoria and Edward Sackville-West had been available in 1931). Ernst Stahl, who knew Leishman, may have discussed the poems with MacNeice. Rilke was much in vogue during and after the War, translations appearing in *Poetry London* and other magazines. The book on Yeats reveals MacNeice's admiration for the German poet, who would have reinforced his conviction about death; he quotes from the *Ninth Elegy*, '... your holiest inspiration's / Death, that friendly Death' (*Yeats*, p. 161). Most important is

MacNeice's interpretation of Rilke's concept of *Verwandlung*, 'transformation':

> Man's gift of seeing is, paradoxically, for Rilke a bridge to the inner invisible world. Sense experience can surmount the senses. Articulation in speech instead of pinning things down can release them from the slavery of the moment. ... As he wrote in the *First Elegy* (Leishman and Spender's translation):
>
> > Yes, the Springs had need of you. Many a star
> > was waiting for you to espy it. Many a wave
> > would rise in the past towards you; or else, perhaps,
> > as you went by an open window, a violin
> > would be giving itself to someone. All this was a trust.
>
> Das alles war Auftrag. Yeats expressed himself differently but he too was ready to vindicate Here and Now as means of canalizing eternal truth.
>
> (*Yeats*, pp. 127-8)

This seems to chime with MacNeice's own ambition, to extract from the finite signs of transcendence, but Rilke—as he pointed out—had experienced a genuine mystical vision to which his work gave expression. MacNeice could manipulate history, previous literature, and natural phenomena to embody his desire for renewal, yet the syntax and imagery are tired. The assertion that these efforts are 'unforced' begins to look like a defence, especially in view of the available drafts.

The poem draws on memories that have intense personal significance: the reference to 'Alison' is particularly connected with the idyllic last term at Marlborough, when MacNeice and Blunt 'would spend whole afternoons lying naked on the grassy banks of the bathing place, eating strawberries and cherries and reciting the *Pervigilium Veneris* or "An hendy hap ichabbe y-hent"'.[4] Although the walled garden has particular medieval associations which he meant to conjure, the combination of wall and wind blowing recurs in MacNeice's poetry, and is undoubtedly rooted in a childhood experience: an extraordinarily vivid concatenation of taste—ginger, sensation—the salt breeze, smell—herring, and the sight of the sea. It was on this same Portstewart holiday that he had a 'revelation of space':

We were walking along a road between high walls and I could see nothing but the road and the air on the road was quiet and self-contained. On the top of

the walls, on the contrary, there were long grasses growing in the stonework
and these were blown out, combed, by a wind which I could not see. I won-
dered what was over those walls and I thought that it must be space. (*Strings*,
pp. 39-40)

The wall becomes both the necessary horizon and the suggestion
of what lies beyond it: as section IV has it, 'What makes in fact
the garden, saves it from not-being' is perhaps also a stepping-
stone:

> So that what is beyond it
> (That which as well perhaps could be called what
>   is Not)
> Is the sanction itself of the wall and so of the garden?
> Do we owe these colours and shapes to something
>   which seems their death?

This is the 'fertilising paradox' central to the poem: space and
enclosure, distance and intimacy, each helps to define the
other.

The idea of the poem and the possibilities of construction
and exploration it suggested were more vivid to MacNeice than
its execution ever conveys. He did not conceive of the genre
clearly enough, despite Rilke's example (or Eliot's): the personal allusions are disguised, losing the force they might have
contributed, and we feel no pressure or urgency in the poem's
advance. This emerges in a comparison of *The Stygian Banks*
with 'Plain Speaking', which adumbrates much of the theme of
the later poem. Both are concerned with language, with the
way context can alter words, with the relation of word to
object. In 'Plain Speaking' MacNeice presents language as
existing in two phases: tautological at the beginning and end of
life, 'entities unfurled' in between. Thus the child identifies the
word with the object—tree, woman—and death cannot turn
into other than itself. In the middle passage words may be
invested with meanings beyond their original capacity—'a tree
becomes / A talking tower, and a woman becomes world'—or,
too flexible, they escape the user, are dulled by repetition, or
become frustratingly inadequate. Yet the experience persists,
whether accurately named or not, even if words are only short-
hand for its occurrence: 'But dream was dream and love was
love ... / And I am I although the dead are dead.' The insistence

is economical. The value of 'Plain Speaking' lies in the irony
the title initiates, a dialectic the poem sets up. *The Stygian Banks*
lapses into assertion rather than illustration, provides signposts
('Making the transient last by having Seen it / And so distilled
value from mere experience') like that capital 'S' which we
might expect MacNeice to avoid. Such defects also mar 'The
North Sea' whose much worked-over drafts, especially of the
final stanza, are matched by the laboriousness of the finished
version (Texas).

The dominating event of the late forties for MacNeice was his
visit to India. While the above poems still bear an imprint of
war, India forced him to look at an entirely different crisis,
challenged assumptions from a new angle. The BBC dispatched
MacNeice and Wynford Vaughan Thomas at the time of Par-
tition, autumn 1947. Vaughan Thomas, in his contribution to
the *Radio Portrait*, said how surprised he was by his orderly,
detached companion's immediate attraction 'to that vast
muddle we call Indian life' (p. 16). MacNeice produced three
radio programmes about India, many of his poems touch on it,
and there is also a prose piece, obviously culled from *India at
First Sight*, called 'The Crash Landing' (*Botteghe oscure*, iv, 1949).
In this, the voice of the Visitor brushes aside the comparisons
offered by the Nanny, the Missionary, and the Uncle (pukka
sahib) which threaten to tame the continent's impact: 'I don't
want any tips from you vested interests, I want to forget all my
own preconceptions—everything I've heard and read' (p. 380).
The Still Voice warns that 'enmeshed in your own background'
it is impossible to 'start from scratch', but MacNeice can at
least enumerate aspects of the country's fantastic diversity.
    In the first poem to emerge from the experience, 'Letter
from India: for Hedli', MacNeice conveys not his delight but
his appalled shock: 'This was the truth and now we see it, /
This was the horror—it is deep'. The beauty of South India
was entirely overshadowed by the Punjab massacres; Vaughan
Thomas and MacNeice had witnessed the aftermath of one:
'I have seen Sheikhupura High School / Fester with glaze-eyed
refugees'. The letter records the distance any traveller feels
from what is familiar and loved, and more, the clash of cultures
that seems to set 'Western assurance' at nothing. MacNeice's

personal resolution of the problem is graceful but not wholly believed in.

The poem's draft (Texas) shows that MacNeice was anxious to discard any intolerance, any Western frame of reference that might foil his attempt to communicate the alien quality of India. So in the second stanza, for example, his setting makes his wife's 'remote so that even lust / Can take no tint or curve on trust / Beyond these plains' beyondless margin': 'beyond-less', while awkward, aptly expresses this particular revelation of space, and it replaces the loaded 'unhallowed'. This is the Forsterian experience of India, confounded by age, expanse, multiplicity, seeing the 'measureless under / Pretended measure'.

The distance that bulks between the continents, and between husband and wife, gives Hedli MacNeice only a fairy-tale reality, 'Beauty asleep in a Grimm story'. A sleeping girl surrounded by thorns is an image of which MacNeice was rather fond; he uses it in connection with his first wife, for example, in *Autumn Journal*:

> Inaccessible in a sleeping wood
> But thorns and thorns around her
> And the cries of night
> And I have no knife or axe to hack my passage
> Back to the lost delight.
>
> (Canto XI)

Here it is a way to slide back into a European framework, a quasi-metaphysical wedding, 'in either [of us] / An India sleeps below our West'. Nevertheless, finding harmony in personal relationships is a retreat from the dilemma the poem poses, and MacNeice cannot solve that.

He is naturally more at ease with learning, cultural assimilation, bypassing the 'things that creep'. This is not to judge MacNeice; as Vaughan Thomas related, where he could act to relieve misery, he did so directly and efficaciously. Perhaps poetry can never cope with mass suffering, unless to satirize those who occasion it. He was not only fascinated but genuinely moved by India. Among notes for an autobiographical lecture given in Cape Town (Berg), he mentioned his 'Irish father's respect for poetry' and scribbled 'cf. India', an unexpected link. In 'India and England 1952', possibly a radio script (Texas), MacNeice wrote of his emotional sympathy with the country, and claimed that it had supplied some lost part of himself. More sceptically, he said in a review of Edward Lear's *Indian Journals* that India, 'being too large and too complex to be "comprehended", invites us to select from her vastness only our own pet properties, rediscovering in fancy dress things we have always fancied'.[5]

'Mahabalipuram' displays this sense of discovery: 'these are the dreams we have needed'. Near Madras, the place was once the chief seaport of the Pallava dynasty, a great trading people. In the seventh and early eighth centuries they carved the coastal granite outcrop with giant reliefs, and sculpted cave temples. On the outskirts of Madras there is also the Portuguese church of the Little Mount, dedicated to St. Thomas who is believed to have reached India. MacNeice jotted down a brief note of what he had seen at both sites (Texas); he did not develop the contrast until he wrote *Didymus* (*Ten Burnt Offerings*), starting at once with the prolific images Mahabalipuram offered him: the massive relief of the Ganges' descent to earth; adjacent boulders with carvings from Hindu mythology; four free-standing temples carved from one long boulder; the Shore Temple built up of granite blocks with one cell opening directly on to the sea, spray from the Indian Ocean eroding the carving. There were so many confrontations: land with sea, rock with wind, natural and aesthetic manifestations of the infinite; now east with west and words with vision.

As he had done in previous poems, MacNeice thought of a questioning opening: 'Why does the shrine face the sea (as the / sphinx faces the desert)? / The lingam alone in the dark cell standing up / to the spray from Australia'; again he realized that such comparisons were better avoided, dulling the impact. When he began again, closer this time to the finished version, he noted alongside the lines:

> All alone from his dark
>   sanctum
>   fronts affronts)
> the lingam faces   )the sea

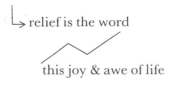

└→ relief is the word

this joy & awe of life

Thus the ending was set, and the predominant impression registered. The lingam fronts the sea, affronts its power yet images it, being like the sea, both creator and destroyer. Mac-Neice's apprehension of the sculpture is untrained, instinctive; he counsels the abandonment of Western categories in the face of the Hindu world (the 'ultra-violet' and 'infra-red' come from his reading of Koestler's *The Yogi and the Commissar*, where they stand for Change from Within and Without): 'look without trying to learn and only look in the act of leaping / After the sculptor into the rockface'. The first draft couches the excitement in short lines; the form the poem eventually took, five long unrhymed lines with two short rhyming ones reflects the multitude of figures to be gathered in, an expansion and the contraction that makes the whole graspable. MacNeice succeeds in expressing the great swirl of movement caught in stone: the eight-armed Durga, for instance, who bears down on the buffalo-headed Demon. He tried 'sculptured turmoil', rejected it for 'wild reliefs', decided to save any mention of relief for the play on the word at the end, and specified: 'the rockhewn windmill / That brandishes axe and knife', rhyming this destruction with the stanza's last line, 'Behold what a joy of life'. The sculptures have been described as having the elongated elegance characteristic of Pallavan art: 'It is as if the action took place behind a gossamer screen which expands with the straining forms but always holds them to a constant plane.'[6] This effect MacNeice captures, yet when he arrives at a summing-up, it is as if his force has been blunted by the surge of words:

> But the visitor must move on and the waves assault
>   the temple,
> Living granite against dead water, and time with
>   its weathering action
>   Make phrase and feature blurred;
> Still from to-day we know what an avatar is, we have
>   seen

God take shape and dwell among shapes, we have
    felt
Our ageing limbs respond to those ageless limbs in
    the rock
    Reliefs. Relief is the word.

In 'Letter from India' he had complained of crossing letters,
'Each answer coming late and little, / The air-mail being no
avatar'. From grumbling over the impossible MacNeice has
moved on to marvel at genuine incarnation. Fumbling at first,
'How men have made rocks become gods become man, we
have felt / The rock in our flesh respond to the flesh in those
rocks', he found a more satisfactory manner of communicating
the element of mystery in the sculptors' handling of the rock,
and the sensual element of his own response. The final sentence
hints at eroticism as well as the intellectual/emotional achievement of comprehension.

'The Crash Landing' has a penultimate statement by the
Still Voice: 'Ambiguity, continuity, perpetuity' (p. 385). It may
have been with these broad themes in mind that MacNeice
wrote to Eliot: 'I am also planning a long poem (about the
length of "Autumn Journal" but much more tightly knit)
which would not be so much "about" India as suggested by
India ... ' (9 February 1948). In a letter of 1 June 1948, he concluded that it was not taking shape, by which time he was
probably working on 'The Window', which he had begun
drafting in the same notebook as 'Mahabalipuram'.

In 1948/9 strength for his own work would have been siphoned
off by *Faust*, whose creatively taxing translation for radio he
undertook with Ernst Stahl. This is generally considered an
extraordinary feat, although Stahl later distinguished between
the strict versification and the lyrics—which he thought could
not have been bettered—and the parts where 'Goethe is slack
or loose in poetic style, and Louis perhaps went too far in following [him]' (*Radio Portrait*, p. 17). This may have had its
repercussions in the longer poems of the fifties, by which time
MacNeice was beginning to register failure: personal, metaphysical, poetic. When he collected his poems in 1949, the
dedicatory poem to his wife expressed only dissatisfaction with
his achievement, leaving no room for the misinterpretation that

these words might be modest disclaimers. He admitted to
'having lived, and too much, in the present, / Askance at the
coming gods, éstranged from those older / Who had created my
fathers in their image'. The one certainty he finds is the existence of 'the Word, like a bulb', some creative touchstone of
truth at present buried. The expression of his unhappiness is
quite plain:

> At one time I was content if things would image
> Themselves in their own dazzle, if the answers
> Came quick and smooth ...
>
> But now I am not content, the leaves are turning
> And the gilt flaking from each private image ...

His poetic solution was to establish a discursive style for his
meditations. During the War he had written a great many
short poems from an altered perspective, his always intense
sensuous impressions sharpened by daily tension. Afterwards
he perhaps felt the need to consolidate intuitions, attach them
to some philosophic spine. The desire to bring into coherent
relation the sense of flux and an essential stability must have
been deepened by his Indian experience, and by the current
uncertainties in British society. There are traces, too, of the
emotional unease that was to prevail in the 1950s, in MacNeice's
seeking to fortify his trust in personal relations.

'The Window' begins with what the Texas draft specifies as
a French painting of flowers at a window as a symbol of sus-
pended equilibrium. We might imagine a canvas similar to
Dufy's *Open Window at St. Janet* in the Tate, or without the
French constraint, Graham Sutherland's 1933 poster 'London
Transport Opens a Window on London's Country', whose
colour and composition match MacNeice's sketch. MacNeice
expatiates on the unperturbed condition of art, a stasis requiring
the spectator's connivance. In the painting there is the room's
interior and the open window, neither space impinging on the
other but fruitfully balanced by the artist; in the final version
the painting itself does not appear until the second stanza.

When he copied out the draft of the first stanza in another
notebook, MacNeice added a list of nine headings, beginning
with 'The Painting' and including 'The Sportsman', 'The
Lover', 'The Workers'. He seems to have had in mind broad

themes of vision, harmony, and everyday life, and to have plotted out this method of embodying them. MacNeice's concern for the architecture of his poems is shown in this kind of planning; that he abandoned the scheme indicates his willingness to be more flexible. It reveals a wish not only to convey the fascination of surface, of incidental details, but also to generalize from some moral core by providing 'types', thus giving reign in poetry to the leaning towards parable which he exploited in broadcasting.

MacNeice wanted 'not merely a formal pattern' in a poem, but also 'the sort of internal structure which will creep in willy-nilly if a poet has some positive values'.[7] In 'The Window' the image of the bridge, and the authority of the artist to place it, is the lynch-pin of the structuring belief. Interestingly, MacNeice does not differentiate here between the gifts of visual and verbal artists: as in 'The National Gallery', the vital function of any art is to 'purge our particular time-bound unliving lives', to fling open windows. The structure with which he was concerned emerges easily in the last stanza of section II, with the assertion of a battered belief; the window reappears as a means of communication, no longer locking watched and watcher in their own worlds. The image draws strength from its biblical and fairy-tale associations.

> Loss and discovery, froth and fulfilment, this is our
>   medium,
> A second best, an approximate, frameless, a sortie,
>   a tentative
> Counter attack on the void, a launching forth from
>   the window
> Of a raven or maybe a dove
> And we do not know what they will find but gambling
>   on their fidelity
> And on other islanded lives we keep open the
>   window and fallibly
> Await the return of love.

Taking its cue from this patience, the opening of section III has lost the exclamatory impatience of section II and become a meditative question, which in the next stanza is replaced by affirmation. Not that the mystery can be elucidated, except tangentially: 'that which art gleaning, congealing, / Sets in antithesis to life / Is what in living we lay claim to'. The gentleness of the ending evades all the questions; it is nearly the gentleness of resignation because the poet places himself inside the room, with the air blowing in. When 'Order to View' (1940) ends, 'And all the curtains flew out of / The windows; the world was open', the poet is outside, everything invites and thus invigorates him.

In 1949 Faber and Faber published MacNeice's *Collected Poems 1925-1948*. His reputation had begun to slide: the *TLS* dismissed the book as showing 'small talent and limited achievement'.[8] The early 1950s seem in retrospect subdued years for the reception of poetry. The War boom was over, and magazines began to disappear: *Poetry Quarterly, Horizon, Poetry London*; *Penguin New Writing*, whose print order had been 100,000 in 1946, dropped to 40,000 by 1949, and was discontinued in 1950. Nevertheless, the period saw 'the emergence of a really new attitude to poetry', according to G. S. Fraser in his introduction to *Poetry Now*.[9] Fraser labelled the thirties' poets 'Augustans'; they were succeeded by 'romantics', who in the fifties lost ground to Amis, Wain, and company: an 'ousting of the bohemians by the pedants'. MacNeice objected to this kind of grouping on principle: 'As individuals then, we must welcome some of these New Liners, but as a group or a Movement, well, let them go. And behold, they go—with what docile arrogance, with what lowered but polished sights; roped together, alert for falling slates, they scale their suburban peaks —the Ascent of C3.' He had no objection to lucidity and neatness, holding that any professional should be able to employ these qualities at will, but his sympathies went to poets subject to 'creative seizures': W. S. Graham and W. R. Rodgers, for instance. Poets should dare, he had remarked some years before, to return to 'Shakespeare's catholic receptivity' ('Images', p. 126). This was hardly the fashionable line.

MacNeice claimed that his own most recent volume broke new ground: '... these poems being more architectural—or perhaps I should say symphonic—than what I was doing before'.[10] In the introduction to his own selection of *Eighty-Five Poems* (1959), he still maintained that *Ten Burnt Offerings* was his best book. Although the *TLS* reviewer was non-committal, noting the change of poetic form and characterizing it as a 'meditative exercise in poetic apprehension', the poems had an extremely enthusiastic and sympathetic reception from W. S. Merwin in the *Kenyon Review*.[11]

These poems were written in Greece, where MacNeice was attached to the British Council in Athens, from March 1950 to March 1951. When they were published in 1952, they were prefaced with a verse revealing a much fiercer attitude to the poet's craft than was shown in 'The Window' ('Then let the poet ... be proudly humbled / And jettison his doubt'):

> Every voyage is a death,
> Every action is a loss,
> Every poem drees its weird,
> Carries its meaning like a cross;
> Yet the burnt poet loves the fire
> Which gulps what pittance he can give—
> Dry words dying, dying, dead,
> Burning that the Word may live.

Each poem is in four 'movements', one of which is usually unbroken. MacNeice called them 'experiments in dialectical structure' (*Poetry Book Society Bulletin*, May 1957). Such a structure is particularly clear in the *Suite for Recorders*, where it operates in the alternations of pastoral and violence; in *Areopagus*, with its tension between ancient and Christian beliefs; in *Cock o' the North*, which explores the myth and the actual life of Byron, himself plagued by conflict; and in *Didymus*, which plays on the same contrasts as 'Mahabalipuram', further complicated by the introduction of Thomas the Doubter. There are few structural parallels, but the poems are linked by recurrent imagery, especially of water. Where this is absent, in *The Death of a Cat*, there are other echoes: for instance the description of the cat, 'Fluid as Krishna chasing the milkmaids', matches evocations of Indian gods in *Didymus*; the words of Gauguin in *Our Sister Water*—'Now a metre of green being, as a Frenchman said, / Greener than a centimetre'—connect with the knowledge 'that green grass / Is more than grass or green' in *Cat*. That and *Flowers in the Interval* are the lightest and most charming poems, chains of graceful similes, needing no other argument than praise. MacNeice can absolutely indulge his pleasure in sensuously charged words: in *Modern Poetry*, apropos of 'Fear No More', he had admitted that 'even now words like "gold" and "roses" tend to strike me as if written in block capitals, and in writing myself I have to avoid playing to this primitive reaction ... ' (p. 43). In *Flowers* he uses his sleeping-princess-in-a-thicket image with a romantic variation, 'a quickset hedge of fiddlebows', and spends the entire third movement luxuriating in comparisons: 'Because your colours are onyx and cantaloupe, / Wet seaweed, lizard, lilac, tiger-moth / And olive groves and beech-woods ...'.

While the *Suite* and *Cock o' the North* deploy considerable scholarship, wearing it lightly (and MacNeice gently mocks it in *Cat*: '... The Greek Anthology / Laments its pets (like you and me, darling), / ... / Those poets were late though. Not really classical'), *Day of Returning* makes use of classical myth in a more personal way, linking it in conception with *Day of Renewal*. When MacNeice sent the poems to London for broadcasting, he wrote a long explanatory letter to the producer Terence Tiller, which was then used as a basis for the introductions (21 April 1951. Texas). He indicated that the opening lines of *Returning* III—'But even so, he said, daily I hanker, daily / Ache to get back to my home, to see my day of returning'—were an approximate translation of his key text from the *Odyssey* and that the poem counterpointed Odysseus and Jacob, 'both "practical" men—in spite of their supernatural digressions'. The idea of home was central: 'variations on home proper, "home from home", and home beyond the sky etc.' This returns to an old preoccupation, no doubt deepened by the years of travelling for the BBC and the sojourn in Athens: 'We are all homeless sometimes, homesick sometimes'. MacNeice is best when he composes Odysseus' meditations on the seductions of Calypso, whose perfection falls short of the real challenges of Ithaca; nostalgia for a grittier way of life, for the sight of remembered seas.

Merwin was particularly excited by the extension in range these poems showed, beyond MacNeice's previously limited personae; *Didymus*, he thought, was the most impressive. MacNeice here chose a subject exactly suited to his gifts and his own quandaries: he could verbally imitate the metaphysical tension between the One and the Many. Thus the opening section describes the Mahabalipuram shrine, enacts the Indian 'riot of dialectic', both aesthetic and human, with which Thomas was confronted. The second pits against the confusion Thomas's simplicity, 'With his two hands and his cruse of doubt / Which never ran dry', figured in the austere church of the Little Mount. Simplicity and doubt coexist in Thomas, who is not given to tortuous analysis but to elementary questioning:

> Was he that once, the sole delight of my soul?
> My memory wilts in the heat. I was mending a net
> When I sensed with a start that I was under his eye
> And he called my name; the rest of his words I
> forget.

The homophones, occurring in the first or third line of each stanza in III, emphasize his dubiety: words that are apparently the same with quite different meanings, identity and disparity. Part IV expands once more into evocation of the Indian landscape, interrupted by two eight-line sections in couplets, like the voices of tempters challenging the saint and the poet himself. The former presumably, and the latter deliberately, come to rest on the same finality: 'On a bare plaque the bare but adequate tribute / To one who had thrust his fingers into the wounds of God.'

Yet the solution for MacNeice is only poetically possible. He asks sombrely in *Day of Renewal*: 'Do I prefer to forget it? / This middle stretch of life is bad for poets;' back then to autobiography, and 'instead of high-powered myths (e.g. Meleager, Calypso) Whittington and nursery rhymes' (letter to Tiller). The second section where these predominate is the least successful. MacNeice is better with the wistfully personal, places, emotions and birthdays linked inextricably, spread out like browned photographs for him to puzzle out the connection between the man in 'Lahore / Blood, cholera, flies, blank eyes, becoming forty', the man of forty three 'At sea in the small hours heading west', and the child told 'that ten was a ripe

age / When presents must be useful'. The thread he finds is the
season of his birth, time for bonfires:

> For all my years are based on autumn,
> Blurred with blue smoke, charred by flame,
> Thrusting burnt offerings on a god
> Who cannot answer to his name.

The last stanza proffers a less melancholy conclusion: perhaps
in the end 'through blown smoke' there will drift 'a god who
needs no name'.

Voluminous drafts for *Ten Burnt Offerings* (Texas) and *Autumn
Sequel* (Texas and the Berg Collection) attest to the immense
trouble MacNeice went to in writing them. The latter was a
strategy of despair, a way of working through a barren period.
MacNeice's account of its inception supplies the key to its
eventual failure. To use Merwin's distinction, this is 'material
to be worked-up' not, as in the case of *Ten Burnt Offerings*,
'access to new command and new *subject* to command' (p. 475).

After that sequence, MacNeice faltered into silence. Extremely depressed, in August 1953 he 'suddenly and quite
cold-bloodedly decided to write another long poem hinged
to an autumn season', which would be called *Autumn Sequel*.
'... changes in the world and changes in my own poetic aims
have made the sequel a more calculated and less occasional
work than its predecessor', he admitted in the introduction to
the first broadcast programme of the poem's early cantos (28
June 1954). Whereas public events in 1938 had dictated the
flow of *Autumn Journal*:

> In 1953 public events, rightly or wrongly, failed to inspire me in the same
> way. *Autumn Sequel*, however, is not, I would say, a private poem. There are
> certain themes running through it, often presented in a mythical form, which
> throughout history have been the stock-in-trade not only of poets but of all
> thinking men—perhaps I should say of all brooding men. The point of *Autumn
> Sequel* is the wedding of myth and topicality, ... while the newspaper material
> is greatly diminished, there is a corresponding increase in the topical human
> element.

The idea of such a poem, although only realized in 1953, seems
to have occurred to MacNeice nearly a decade before. When he
sent Eliot some revised proofs for *Springboard*, he wrote that he

did not expect to produce another volume of short poems for a considerable time, having in mind a long poem that might take years to shape:

I can't tell you much about this project at the moment except (1) that the main characters will be imagined contemporary individuals, but will exist on two planes, i.e. the symbolic as well as the naturalistic. (2) That there will be some inter-shuttling of past and present (though in a much more modified way than Ezra Pound's Cantos). (3) That the total pattern will be very complex, and in fact rather comparable to the 'Faerie Queene' in its interlocking of episodes, sub-plots, and digressions which aren't really digressions.

(7 April 1944)

Connolly judged the poem to be more ambitious than *Autumn Journal*, 'loosely constructed round the portrait of a group of friends like Elgar's Enigma Variations'.[12] Some are easily identifiable: Gwilym as Dylan Thomas, Gavin as Graham Shepard, Egdon as Auden. For MacNeice, who details in the poem the pressures working for disillusionment, conformity, anonymity, despair, who finds death coming prematurely to many, his friends are the bearers of value in his world. It may be courage or humour, kindness or wit that marks them out; most importantly, they may have rescued a pattern from the encroaching formlessness. MacNeice's scepticism did not include the people he had accepted as friends; reluctant to commit himself, he was tenacious once he had done so, 'a great cherisher of friendships'.[13] Spender has remarked of the portrait of Dylan Thomas that it is 'brilliant and vivid and produces exactly the effect which Dylan himself wanted to produce' (*Books and Bookmen*, August 1975, p. 21). MacNeice lacks Yeats's confidence in making heroes of his friends, nor does he hold the doctrine of the mask which gives a role its *raison d'être*. He praises integrity but can only describe the external show. The next year MacNeice adapted *The Waves*, which he saw as a long prose poem, 'elegiac and yet defiant'. He quoted Bernard in a note for the *Radio Times*: 'We have proved, sitting eating, sitting talking, that we can add to the treasury of moments' (11 March 1955, p. 5). This, he felt, was characteristic of Bloomsbury; it is also close to his attitude in the *Sequel*, an appreciation of friends who could enrich each other's lives simply by being together, though some were trying to create things more lasting than conversation. MacNeice's poem is elegiac by virtue of the dead it commemorates; its length and range make sustained intensity impossible.

The knowledge that he set about writing *Autumn Sequel* so deliberately accords with our reading of the poem: it seems wilful, contrivance is sometimes painfully apparent. The very first canto, in which MacNeice proliferates the clichés, tags, colloquialisms he feels have the power to excite, fails on those terms.[14] August is the opening month for *Autumn Journal* also, and MacNeice makes constant reference to the earlier poem, 'scrawled on the sky / In my hand of unformed smoke'; remembering the exhilaration lacing it, and the comment to Eliot that it contained everything of importance in his life, the weariness of this Canto I seems even more dispiriting: 'It is not time I resent, it is that the hand should stick / On a lie which the heart repeats again and again.' The brief salute to Wimbush (Gordon Herrickx, who was a stonemason by day, sculptor by night), chiselling 'his vision in a midland shed/ Chip upon chip, undaunted and unknown', (I), the panegyric to Graham Shepard (II), indicate that if MacNeice did not resent the passage of time, he was certainly obsessed by it. Like Eliot's publican in *The Waste Land*, MacNeice has his park-keepers call 'All Out', their whistles sounding for closing time. Unlike Eliot, he is not content to let the command stand, but must explain:

> A harsh voice cries All Out—all out of Regent's Park,
> Of Everest, of Eden—casts a doubt
> If we were ever in. The whole massif is dark,
>
> The one tree silent, one day (to-day) ruled out, all
>   out.
>
> (Canto III)

By such symbols: the Fall, fall; the Tree—of knowledge, the Cross; expulsion and subsequent search for a home, the cantos are linked. MacNeice creates his own myths: the climbing of Everest (he wrote a commentary for a film on the subject), which is part of the Quest theme but appealed to him particularly for Mallory's reason, 'because it is there'; the 'Parrot', who appears periodically as a symbol of mechanical civilization, and is related to the betraying Cock. There is also, of course, the unification provided by the *terza rima* form; the trick of connecting one section with the next by means of last and first lines had already been practised in *The Stygian Banks*.

Notes for *Autumn Sequel* in the Berg Collection witness to MacNeice's thorough planning, down to a list of reference books marked according to their relevant cantos: Willey's *Seventeenth-Century Background*, for instance, for the one on Norwich (XVI); for the last two cantos a guide to Ravenna and *The Oxford Book of Carols*. To manipulate themes and connections throughout the *Sequel* involved pages of key phrases assigned to later cantos and paired with earlier ones, a check kept on months and dates appropriate to certain places and people.

MacNeice may have treasured most his version of the Quest —cantos XIV, XV, XVI—which he found a perenially interesting theme, but because of their relaxed coherence the two Oxford cantos, XII and XIII, read better, with their affectionate portraits of Boyce (E. R. Dodds) and Aloys (Ernst Stahl); and for sustained insight, there is the impressive Canto XXII about Sherborne and Marlborough. As D. B. Moore remarks, a concern with himself is the least prevalent theme of *Autumn Sequel*, and this canto is an unusually shrewd piece of self-analysis. What makes it the most notable of the whole sequence is the recounting of the dream MacNeice had at Marlborough (see also *Strings*, p. 101). This was the appalling vision of the Crucifixion occurring as part of a tawdry fun-fair; MacNeice breasts the hill and sees it all in a hollow, knowing his father is climbing behind, 'and through the noise I foresaw the world collapse // In my father's mind in a moment'.

The structure that would emerge willy-nilly from belief is absent from the poem. MacNeice writes about his wife's preparations for Christmas Eve and gallantly puts aside 'chill and sallow thoughts':

> While I, brought up to scoff rather than bless
> And to say No, unless the facts require
>
> A neutral verdict, for this once say Yes.
>
> (Canto XXIV)

He prays in the last canto that each of his friends might have 'the fruits of his desire', travels homeward in the company of visionaries, Blake, Aristotle, perhaps the Kings, towards one 'who takes the ancient view that life is holy'. 'But if I were asked whether this were a Christian poem, I should not know what to reply. All I know is that I have been saturated from my childhood in Christian symbolism and that some of these symbols seem to me still most valid' (introduction to the sixth broadcast, 1 August 1954). So it appears in the poem, the newly constructed symbols carrying little weight of conviction and experience. It seems an immensely sad work, so laboured over and so little satisfying. The unmoving traveller carried to his destination is much more despairing than the man who protested against injustices he could not right, in *Autumn Journal*, but who felt he could himself take a new, more honest direction. At the outset of the later poem MacNeice accepted, even welcomed, contradiction, in Whitman's words; he seems to search, nevertheless, for some means of resolution, haunted by not being able to accept his father's. Endeavouring to give almost every object significance, he leaves nothing to that chance he admires in sports, which 'Because they are not foregone, move in fluid borders' (XXIII). The *TLS* reviewer remarked acutely that what we miss in the *Sequel* is the 'sense of an area of unused force outside the poem' (26 November 1954, p. 754). The painstaking plotting affects the poem adversely; it caused MacNeice to obscure the one thing that might have held the poem together: his own observant, striving, desolate, sociable, isolated self.

V. THE LYRIC RETURN

While MacNeice deplored reviewers' misinterpretations of *Autumn Sequel*, he had less to complain of in the reception of *Visitations* (1957). Although critical approval was qualified, it was generally concluded that MacNeice had rejected an aberrant style, the new poems suggesting a fresh development. The lyrical impulse, suppressed in the writing of longer poems, had returned: 'I like to think that my latest short poems are on the whole more concentrated and better organised than my earlier ones, relying more on syntax and bony feature than on bloom or frill or the floating image', he wrote in the *Bulletin* for May 1957.

Nevertheless, earlier poems provide models for *Visitations*. MacNeice's description of the volume matches one he jotted down for *Springboard*, when he was preparing an autobiographical lecture to be given in Cape Town: 'verse more austere & unified—new concentration on syntax, bony structure' (Berg). 'April Fool' from the later book is reminiscent of 'Nuts in May'; 'A Hand of Snapshots' or 'Jigsaws' resembles the sequence 'Novelettes' in *Plant and Phantom*. This rediscovery of a former style is beneficial; the less successful poems have closer antecedents: for instance, 'Donegal Triptych' bears traces of 'The North Sea' and 'The Window'. MacNeice does not quite know how to jettison or modify the style he stabilized with such effort in the 1950s, yet he also anticipates themes and phrases that become striking in his next volume.

The dedication to *Visitations* indicates that MacNeice is ready to bypass topicality, the world interpreted by the media; it had made his *Journal* memorable but had failed in the *Sequel*. In changing 'With all those public *dilemmas* which bruise our minds' to 'fears', he implied that events had passed beyond the point where the reasoning individual could make a contribution; better then for the poet, 'the timeless vagrant', to find and transmit value (Texas; 'To Hedli').

Certainly his way forward seems to be through a constant clarification of the past, a return to scenes to find out what

residue of feeling remains, what might be reawakened or revealed. MacNeice seeks not only sources of value, but also
resources for art. In this way the poems of *Visitations* are connected with *Ten Burnt Offerings*: '... a sombre view / Where
neither works nor days look innocent / And both seem now too
many, now too few' (*Day of Renewal*). Recurrence has been a
matter of nightmare and of vision, more often a guarantee of
hope than of melancholy. In 'Donegal Triptych', however, to
the contention that 'each arrival means returning' he opposes:

> Returning where? To speak of cycles
> Rings as false as moving straight
> Since the gimlet of our fate
> Makes all life, all love, a spiral.

Change, absence, and possession gnaw at him. A Heraclitan
paradox runs 'it stays by changing'. MacNeice is unsure. Can
he perceive the essential familiarity of objects despite change,
and thus convey their nature; are his altered perceptions bound
to falsify what he sees or will they become more accurate with
age? Revisited, Donegal holds its core of fear: 'Youth and
poetry departed.'

MacNeice's choice of style in 'A Hand of Snapshots' may
have been motivated by concern to make his experience less
ostensibly autobiographical, more accessible. The Berg Collection draft of 'The Here-and-Never' (*Visitations*, notebook 4) is
marked by frequent changes of pronouns to distance memories:
in the third stanza, for instance, 'Few were few and we knew
them all' became 'Few were few but all knew all.' These poems
about return are unremittingly bleak, only revelatory of inadequacy and failure. The language is extremely plain. 'The Gone-
Tomorrow' and 'The Here-and-Never' are both about exile
and death, one from the world of childhood, the other from
a familiar community. When MacNeice writes about the
child's apprehension of the world, it is not with his usual nostalgia for that clarity: what matters in this poem is that senses
fail, nature is lost to us:

> And the blaze of whins, the smell of turf,
> The squelch of mud, the belch of surf,
> The slop of porridge, the squawk of gulls,
> Enter that smallest of small skulls.

The last lines of the poem, 'Will all have vanished and the skies / Have lost their blue like those blue eyes', remind us of Yeats's 'The Lover Pleads with His Friend for Old Friends': 'Your beauty perish and be lost / For all eyes but these eyes'; MacNeice allots to memory no such consolatory power. The two dimensions in his poem, of wide landscape and small skull, correspond to those of eternity and now in the more abstractly expressed despondency of 'The Here-and-Never'. MacNeice juggles with a restricted vocabulary in the poem as though to enact human inadequacy to cope with loss; the sequence as a whole has a neatness of construction, balance of assonance or alliteration within lines, end-rhyme or repetition, all severer than he normally imposed. The remark by Auden that Mac-Neice quoted in a review may be relevant to his own practice here: '... the more he (the poet) is conscious of an inner disorder and dread, the more value he will place on tidiness in the work as a defence ...'.[1]

The two poems admitting first-person pronouns are quite different in their tone. 'The Once-in-Passing' employs the familiar symbol of the window; here it is marked with a cross, as in a photograph:

> And here the cross on the window means myself
> But that window does not open;
> Born here, I should have proved a different self.
> Such vistas dare not open;
> For what can walk or talk without tongue or feet?

The riddle goes unanswered. Clearly the open window always signifies in his poems potential, communication, even inspiration. In the last stanza, where the open window is linked with an 'ancient' cross, the nexus seems Christian, a wind blowing in, and that connects with the roots whose lack he laments in stanza two. This is an adult and despairing version of the fabled West. MacNeice wrote 'The Here-and-Never', then 'The Once-in-Passing', then 'The Gone-Tomorrow'; by the order in which he chose to print them he emphasized not the frail hope which closes 'The Once-in-Passing', nor the finality which marks 'The Gone-Tomorrow', but the less acceptable finality of 'The Here-and-Never' which means that return, especially 'to the opened eye' can only involve recognizing its impossibility, in any true sense.

MacNeice goes back to Ireland, also to India and the subjects
of former poems. His perspective is shaped by death, his own
or that of others. There is no bravado, or even acceptance, just
a notation of reverberating fact. He is not yet provoked to unserious and sardonic poetry on the subject.

In the *Bulletin* MacNeice said that he hoped his 'poems of
place' existed on more than one level, though they were 'superficially ... merely descriptive pieces'. Unfortunately the contrasts he points are too obvious in some poems, whose perceptions belong to the radio-travelogue genre: 'Return to
Lahore', for example, or 'Visit to Rouen', concerning the fifth
centenary of the rehabilitation of St. Joan, with its accompanying commercial exploitation. He is better observing Wessex
and Africa, where he registers imperturbable natural forces
working independently of man.

MacNeice went to Africa to obtain material for a document-
ary programme *The Fulness of the Nile* (broadcast 3 July 1955);
the rest-house he wrote about was near Nimule, where the Nile
flows north from Uganda to the southern Sudan. MacNeice
domesticates the river for the English imagination, 'bowling its
agelong bias out of Uganda'; it takes a character akin to
Kipling's Limpopo, 'Tipsy with goggled hippo and drifting
lilies', a line which mimics the constricted then leisurely movement of the water. Thus the element of mystery and a hint of
terror are more potent when they appear in the last stanza:

> The bed beneath the ghostly netting beckoned
> To chrysalid or sepulchral sleep. But such
> Was now the river's dominance that he filtered
> Through even the deepest sleep, weaving his journey
> Out of too little history into too much.

The last line not only encapsulates a British view of the continent's history, but also obliquely involves the dream-laden
sleep, summons shadows of older metaphors in which Africa
was an image of the unconscious.

In 'Wessex Guidebook', too, MacNeice tames the seasons so .
that in the end their real aloofness is more striking. He began
the poem under the title 'Museums' with what became its third
stanza and is—with the first—its strongest (Berg, *Visitations*,
notebook 2). His poems about repositories of 'culture', mu-

seums, art galleries, universities, the BBC (in *Autumn Sequel*),
make an interesting group in the ambiguity of the attitudes
they display. While he was a beneficiary of such institutions,
indeed a transmitter of their values to some extent, their static
quality alarmed MacNeice, and their entrenched isolation
from ordinary lives:

> As here in Oxford shadow the dark-weathered
> Astrakan rustication of the arches
>   Puts a small world in quotes:

He had written 'Puts the whole college in quotes', whereas his
revision catches the self-sufficiency he meant to portray (Texas).
In that poem 'Relics', MacNeice moves from the elegant
(qualified) obsolescence of Oxford—'obsolete as books in
leather bindings'—

> To downs where once without either wheel or hod
> Ant-like, their muscles cracking under the sarsen,
> Shins white with chalk and eyes dark with necessity,
>   The Beaker People pulled their weight of God.

These folk obviously appealed to MacNeice's imagination:
here their effort and passion outweighs the light pinnacles of a
subsequent city; in his radio play *The Queen of Air and Darkness*,
the protagonist is proud of his Beaker ancestry, inherits their
single-minded endurance; and in 'Wessex Guidebook' they
outlast even the Roman occupation, barrows against barracks.
What lasts has not always been intended to do so, thus a museum
is to some degree a freak collection of objects: a flake-tool has
survived, so has a butterfly. In comfortably casing and labelling
them we reveal the pattern we wish to establish, and in our
monuments distort what is preserved. MacNeice sees galleries
as potentially subversive, from which people could emerge with
'a sheaf / Of inklings fluttering in their minds, and now even
the open / Air is half-articulate and unsafe' ('Picture Galleries',
August 1940); or as a refuge for delusion, in which the viewer

> Mirrors himself in the cases of pots, paces himself
>   by marble lives, ...
> And then returns to the street, his mind an arena
>   where sprawls
> Any number of consumptive Keatses and dying Gauls.
>   ('Museums', 1933)

When he writes in 'Wessex Guidebook' of the survival of history, it is in the form of popular myth; where history is ignored, it is the 'homebrewed past' that is despised. Both lopsided views are, however, dwarfed by the movement of 'those illiterate seasons'. MacNeice has an oddly cosy picture of them which becomes stern and measured:

> Still smoke their pipes in swallow-hole and hide-out
> As scornful of the tractor and the jet
> As of the Roman road, or axe of flint,
> Forgotten by the mass of human beings
> Whom they, the Seasons, need not even forget
> Since, though they fostered man, they never loved him.

The original version of the last line, 'Since they have helped them once but never knew them', has been honed to perfection, man's illusion about nature's benignity, or even interest, dismissed with a finality exceeding that achieved by MacNeice in 'Evening in Connecticut' (1940).

Similarly history is discounted, though in favour of a kindlier nature, when he returns to the subject of the British Museum. There history is both personal and impersonal, and the poem would once have included the lines, 'I smoke to postpone return / Into that pantheon of the printed word / Where Marx and Mazzini worshipped' (Berg, *Visitations*, notebook 1), except that MacNeice decided to keep his catalogue general, closer to the spirit of the boy who knew no such names, who

> Prefers to linger here with pigeons and sparrows
> For whom neither truth nor falsehood, heaven nor hell,
> Holds any purport, who have no regrets,
> No ideals and no history—only wings.
>
> ('Time for a Smoke')

MacNeice is searching, throughout *Visitations*, for some means of reconciling disparate experiences to form a continuum which will plot his life. At times he construes one incident— the child running upstairs to beat a hotel lift—as a paradigm of subsequent effort, and in 'Time for a Smoke' he can identify with the child 'come down in a lift which he failed to beat'. More frequently the past is alien territory, and from what happened there nothing can be learnt, although it sometimes speckles a dream or a nightmare. We see these concerns from different angles in the grouping of 'Time for a Smoke', 'Jig-saws', and 'Easter Returns'.

'Jigsaws' was originally called 'Four Puzzles' (Berg, *Visitations, notebook* 1), the second poem being omitted; the change in title emphasizes that each poem is puzzling and that the whole sequence, while it basically concerns one man, can only be fitted together with difficulty. The third poem concentrates on the similarity between man and the 'brutes', after the differences enumerated in 'Time for a Smoke':

> The iceberg of our human lives
> Being but marginal in air,
> Our lonely eminence derives
> From the submerged nine-tenths we share
> With all the rest who also run,
> Shuddering through the shuddering main.

It contrasts sharply with the mocking gaiety of the preceding poem—'Property! Property! Let us extend / Soul and body without end'—which fastens on human acquisitiveness, bourgeois clutter, and the stunted soul. Life seems farcical in the jaunty rhythms and rhymes, but not desperate and naked. The two generalized predicament are flanked by two personal ones, versions of the same question concerning identity. The first—'What ghosts of cuckoo-spit and dew / Veil those fields that I once knew?'—despite its air of being a mere philosophi-cal conundrum, a variation on the tree-in-the-quad debate, is genuinely disquieting, the other even more so: 'Fresh from the knife and coming to / I asked myself could this be I / They had just cut up' (IV). MacNeice recounted the experience of his peritonitis operation in America in *The Strings are False* in almost exactly the poem's phrases, although he had long abandoned the prose manuscript, and the same is true of a later phase of his illness, which he describes in 'The Messiah (a memory of 1940)' (*Strings*, pp. 27-9). This sensation of being a stranger to his own life troubles the poems. Their regular form, the re-assurance of repetition and couplets, gives them an almost nursery-rhyme simplicity crossed with the tone of nonsense poetry, and still the bewilderment leaks out. The attempt in the fifth poem to end with some certainty—'... we know / We need

the unknown. The Unknown is There'—emerges as a palliative,
a way out of the dilemma of belief proffered without much
conviction.

In 'Easter Returns', however, the Christian festival is
allowed to convey some essential truth, correspond to some
visible and invisible movement of grace.

> Further, who failed last Friday to feel grieved,
>   What right have we to this day's joy?
> Whether our childhood stand deceived
>   Or not, the years destroy
> What happened in the garden, bliss or pain.

This stanza carries its religious charge—Eden and Gethsemane
—and its burden of memory: of Bishop MacNeice's sorrow
and joy at Easter, perhaps of his mother weeping as she walked
the garden path, and of himself as a child on Good Friday,
'keeping my face austere, trying not to be pleased by the daf-
fodils' (*Strings*, p. 59). The 'green shooting from the wounded
mind', the secular version of resurrection offered in the poem,
could be an image of the art whose creation stems from pain.
MacNeice reserves his assent.

He was more at ease experimenting with fairy story and
allegory, forms which increasingly occupied his attention.
They were a natural recourse for broadcasting, since the lack of
a visual dimension facilitates fantasy; MacNeice commented in
his Clark Lectures, *Varieties of Parable*, that the medium tempted
him to modern morality of parable plays, 'but only once, I
think, to my own satisfaction'.[2] Possibly that was *The Dark
Tower*, first broadcast on 21 January 1946, to which listeners
responded enthusiastically. In the 1950s, besides various travel
features and poetry programmes, MacNeice wrote *One Eye
Wild, Prisoner's Progress* (which won the Premio d'Italia in
1954), and adapted a Norwegian folk-tale, *East of the Sun and
West of the Moon*.[3] Previewing the first of these in the *Radio
Times*, MacNeice remarked of his 'would-be hero' that he, 'like
many of us today, suffers from the lack of a mythology' (7
November 1952, p. 8). The most acceptable solution to this
problem was to use as the core of his allegories the Quest, in
its various guises. The prisoner tunnels to escape but also
journeys—with the aid of a woman and a fine memory for

verse—towards a Truth he dimly discerns. Helga, in *East of the Sun*, searches for the means to release a Bear/Prince, so Mac-Neice can here combine the quest with the transformation of vision that springs from the recognition of love. When he gave the Clark Lectures, MacNeice admitted that at times he had become a journalist rather than a creative writer, and continued:

In the 1930's we used to say that the poet should contain the journalist; now I would tend more often to use 'contain' in the sense of control or limit... What the poet is far more concerned with is that 'inner conflict'... [requiring] metaphorical writing. So in English poetry I was sorry to see a few years ago that movement which was called the Movement deliberately lowering its sights and concentrating on neat observations within a very limited sphere. ... What I myself would now like to write, if I could, would be double-level poetry, of the type of Wordsworth's 'Resolution and Independence', and, secondly, more overt parable poems in a line of descent both from folk ballads such as 'True Thomas' and some of George Herbert's allegories in miniature such as 'Redemption'. (*Parable*, p. 8)

Although these lectures were delivered in 1963, he was trying his hand at double-level and parable poetry well before that time. George Herbert does not belong to his early pantheon, but in 1944 he wrote 'Prayer Before Birth' on the model of 'Sighs and Grones', and in 1952 and 1954 gave approving reviews of books about Herbert.[4] He subsequently planned a lecture or radio talk on Herbert and Herrick, for which the Berg Collection holds notes.

In the *New Statesman* review MacNeice chose construction as Herbert's first virtue; in the talk he compared his 'order (subtle)' to that of Horace, with its elaborate regular patterns and intricately varied syntax, and quoted Summers concerning 'the attempt to make formal structure an integral part of the meaning'. 'Prayer Before Birth' has these same virtues. On the sleeve of the Argo recording, MacNeice placed the poem at the end of his war phase, in which 'I myself grew more relaxed while my poetry tightened up'. That he was 'much concerned with paradoxes and ironies' also suits his metaphysical model. When he reads the poem, MacNeice hastens through the third stanza, in which the only positive note sounds, and grimly relishes the doom he describes in the fifth: 'my children curse me' has an Ulster harshness. Herbert's petitions in 'Sighs and Grones' are all negative—'O do not fill me', 'O do not kill me!'—until the last stanza; MacNeice reverses this, asking for charity—consolation, provision, a hearing—until his last stanza, whose opening runs 'I am not yet born; O fill me', but closes, 'Otherwise kill me.' The extant draft of the poem (Texas: on notebook leaves, which usually indicates an early version), is written almost without hesitation; if it is a first draft it shows extraordinary control. Like Herbert, he rhymes the first and last lines of the stanzas, runs the first line on to the second, repeats for emphasis in the final stanza. As Herbert considers in each stanza a new punishment that might be visited on him by God, so MacNeice rehearses each stage of the embryo's possible fate. His subtle variation lies in the way one list of disasters is exceeded by the next until the short gasp of the sixth stanza, which repeats the structure of the first and poses two extremes of human behaviour needing no elaboration:

> I am not yet born; O hear me,
> Let not the man who is beast or who thinks he is God
>   come near me.

Whereas the opening is intensely threatening, it is in the fashion of ancient superstition about the effect on the child in the womb of things seen by its mother; in the sixth the warping is both physical and spiritual, and the words have their contemporary political resonance. In a manuscript fair copy of the poem (Texas), MacNeice included an epigraph from Herbert, 'Even poisons praise thee'. It pointed to the paradox the poem's syntax enacts: the unborn child's speech, with its strong and urgent pulse, concerns only what is life-destroying, except in the third stanza. While enumerating methods of grinding destruction, the resistant human will asserts itself. By referring indirectly to Herbert's poems, MacNeice has an added source of irony. In 'Sighs and Grones' the petitioner acknowledges his sins and abases himself, 'But I am frailtie, and already dust', humble before a God who is both '*Cordiall* and *Corrosive*'. In 'Providence' the balance of his creation is hymned, and his
, omnipotence:

> Ev'n poysons praise thee. Should a thing be lost?
> Should creatures want for want of heed their due?
> Since where are poysons, antidotes are most:
> The help stands close, and keeps the fear in view.

In 'Prayer Before Birth' the petitioner is less humble than desperate, the universe is seen to be entirely hostile, at least the brief reference to natural consolations is outweighed by the list of human follies. 'The fear in view' dominates the poem, whose speaker lacks Herbert's certainty that prayer will weigh in the scales.

MacNeice's projected talk illustrates the many voices Herbert could assume, the dramatic openings and endings, hyperbole and surprise, his suggestive simplicity, his use of everyday diction and images drawn from 'something so prosaic as real estate', which he also remarks in *Varieties of Parable* (p. 50). This range of qualities is exercised in 'The Streets of Laredo', in which MacNeice had already achieved the kind of poem whose line of descent he traced in the first Clark Lecture.

In the 1929-34 Notebook there are three poems written to popular tunes; in a notebook compiled *c.*1943 there are adaptations of traditional ballads such as 'Greensleeves', possibly for use in a radio programme (Texas). 'The Streets of Laredo' is a very sophisticated version of such experiments. By imitating the form of the cowboy ballad, and writing about a contemporary event while alluding to historical occasions, MacNeice can play off his direct or oblique allusions against each other without ever having his narrator adopt a particular tone. There is irony and a measure of judgement, but none of the open didacticism of the original. Both are dirges, one for a man and the other for a city. MacNeice's is also the song of a doomed man, since Agag only temporarily survived his people, and was eventually the victim of God's wrath as they had been (I Sam. 15). But that identification was not made originally: the surviving draft of the poem is probably the penultimate one, in which the first line reads: 'O early one morning, my head like a handsaw', is cancelled and replaced by two illegible versions, amongst which 'my liver' is decipherable, and then by the printed form (Texas). That he hit on Agag introduces the idea of fatalism which anyway underpins the poem.

It has been minutely and, on the whole, persuasively analysed by John Irwin in his article 'MacNeice, Auden and the Art Ballad' (*Contemporary Literature*, Winter 1970, pp. 58-79). He identifies MacNeice's biblical sources for the poem, chiefly Revelations, where Babylon is referred to as the golden and fallen city, plainly parallel to London, her great commercial wealth now consumed in the bombing raids. He also points out the aptness of Blake and Bunyan's appearance, who were both much concerned in their work with symbolic cities as a means of conveying contemporary moral dissolution.

The two points at which I would diverge from Irwin's interpretation are in stressing the verve of MacNeice's poem, and casting doubt on the moral judgement Irwin is sure MacNeice is passing. Unlike the cowboy ballad, which becomes slower and slower and has a uniformly lamenting tone, 'The Streets of Laredo' does not slacken its pace until the appearance of the Angel, whose very whisper is triumphant. The first draft of the fourth stanza ran:

> Then out from a doorway there sidled a cockney,
> A rocking-chair rocking on top of his head:
> 'O fifty-five years have I lived in Laredo
> But now I've no home I'd sooner be dead'.

but was altered to the printed version:

> ...
> 'O fifty-five years I been feathering my love-nest
> And look at it now—why, you'd sooner be dead'.

The picture has a surrealistic quality; the anarchy of a bombed landscape was often described and photographed. The simple pathos of the earlier version has been replaced by complexity as well as a livelier turn of speech; the man's efforts are seen to have been futile from the beginning, and his drawing in the spectator reminds us that the latter's immunity is limited. MacNeice does not dwell on this loss nor on the plight of the refugees in the seventh stanza: sensitive perhaps to possible criticism, he altered the second line from '"As enemy alien," says ~~Schwemstein, Baalam,~~ Aron the Jew' to "Says Tom Dick and Harry the Wandering Jew". 'They tell me report at the first police station / But the station is pancaked—so what can I do?' Irwin is right to see in this choice of detail MacNeice's distaste for authority; we may go further and interpret the tone of the whole poem as partaking of that exhilaration at destruction found in 'Brother Fire'. Whether the moral of the poem can be summarized as Irwin suggests is more questionable. He maintains that MacNeice is saying destruction is paid for by destruction; if England had stood by other people when they were bombed—particularly Spain (thinking of Laredo as a Spanish rather than a Texan town)—and had not been concerned with feathering her own nest, this punishment would not have been visited upon her. Given the biblical parallels MacNeice establishes, this is conceivable. Irwin's final contention, however, that the older naïve romanticism of the cowboy ballad is played off against the irony of the modern one, and that in so doing MacNeice judges an earlier moral framework which by implication led to the contemporary moral state, is driving his argument too far. The business of ballad, before the slightly corrupted form it assumed, was never to judge, merely to narrate. This is not to deny that MacNeice used the original dirge ironically in his powerful poem.

When he returned to the mode in *Visitations*, it was less spectacular, more traditional in conception and execution. The quatrains of 'The Burnt Bridge' are patterned a-b-a-c; the last line's not rhyming deadens it, except for the one stanza ending with a question, so that each stage of the story seems self-contained. This is in keeping with the ancient ballad technique of a rapid series of scenes rather than continuous narration (MacNeice's 'Laredo' is more traditional in this respect than the cowboy ballad), whose skill lies in the juxtaposition and selection of events, as may be seen in 'Sir Patrick Spens'. The quest in 'The Burnt Bridge' thus appears a random affair, unpurposeful; that MacNeice intended his protagonist not to be in command of his progress, he shows by revising the third line: 'As he took quick strides to ~~seek~~ tempt his fate' (Texas). The poem has a ballad's economy of vocabulary, rhyme, and frequent alliteration, which are intended to lull the reader into acceptance, to maintain his interest without distracting it. Scant revisions made by MacNeice in the available draft are to quicken the pace of the narrative. He had opened the poem, 'When he had passed through the rustic gate'; the change to 'So, passing through ...' assumes a previous history, and strengthens the impression of the protagonist's impetuosity. Its tentative title had been 'Third Son's Progress' and by the ninth stanza, with the wood safely traversed, the dragon in abeyance, and a lady won, the fairy-tale luck of the third son seems to have held. By choosing to call it instead 'The Burnt Bridge', MacNeice emphasized the only decisive action, and the lack of certainty in a superficially fairy-tale ending:

> So, far they came and found no shore,
> The waves falling, the night falling.
> To board a ship sunk years before,
> And all the world was daylight.

With slight variations, the first and last lines match the opening: does this mean some dragon still has to be vanquished, that the finding of love is only a beginning, that paradise soon ends (the Miltonic echo in the tenth stanza is surely intentional) or that it has no end? The ballad's cadences are reassuring but the situation is unresolved. MacNeice, true to the tradition, draws no moral.

He is prepared to be explicit in his allegory 'Figure of Eight' and in 'The Tree of Guilt', still tentative in 'Visitations'. Death seems a more vivid presence to him than moments of illumination. As 'Death of an Old Lady' records, on his step-mother's dying MacNeice had really heard the banshees: 'At five in the morning there were grey voices / Calling three times through the dank fields'.

The warning cries from shadows are countered by other voices from the heart of light, heard in 'the indefinable moment' ('Visitations' II), not so much encounters as presences briefly apprehended: it is patient alertness that bears fruit. MacNeice may be articulating his own plight in *Visitations* when he writes in section six of the title sequence about hte 'unimmediately apparent' which is in fact the awaited Muse:

> So those who carry this birthright and this burden
> Regardless of all else must always listen
> On the odd chance some fact or freak or phantom
> Might tell them what they want, might burst the cordon
> Which isolates them from their inmost vision.

The phantom for MacNeice turned out to be an unexpected love affair. Davin, among others, refers to it as the source of 'one of those rare bursts of creativity when the poet is first astonished and then alarmed by the way the mill goes on grinding', as MacNeice recalled in the *Bulletin* for February

1961. *Solstices* (1961) carries the epigraph '...age iam meorum / finis amorum' from Horace's *Odes*, IV.11. The volume has much in common with *Visitations*, but MacNeice found that 'fewer of these later poems strike me as forced (in revising I eliminated one or two compulsive bits of trickery) and more of them seem to be "given"' (*Bulletin*). An example of such elimination is to be found in the typed manuscript of 'The Park' (Texas), where 'avoid the void' in the second stanza is altered to 'ignore the void' and similarly in the third stanza 'No pause for their paws' is changed to 'No rest ...'.

The preceding chapter noted the problem posed for MacNeice by his own facility; seeing 'material for poetry everywhere' meant that he shunned few topics. There is sometimes a clear discrepancy between the verbal gifts and formal skill MacNeice deploys, and the inconsequentiality of the resulting poem. Although a just critic of his earliest work, MacNeice was generally loathe to prune or jettison. In *Solstices*, however, he achieves harmony between his intention and the effect it creates, taking pleasure in the tight technical control of the 'Nature Notes' sequence for example, which Auden chose as illustration of MacNeice's excellence in the sixties (*Radio Portrait*, pp. 22-3).

Tentatively assessing his own development for the *Bulletin*, MacNeice said:'... I have become progressively more humble in the face of my material and therefore less ready to slap poster paint all over it. I have also perhaps ... found it easier than I did to write poems of acceptance (even of joy) though this does not—perish the thought—preclude the throwing of mud or of knives when these seem called for.' He cocks a snook at the export of English literature and its patent absurdities in the colonies. Having seen both India and Ghana gain independence, he had finished with any idea of 'the static globe'; no doubt his British Council experience in Athens, and 'continually receiving unexpected deputations from eager young poets' as Vaughan Thomas reported of their Indian trip, sharpened MacNeice's sense of incongruity:

> Shakespeare flaunts his codpiece at dhoti,
> Ditto at sari, Pope with his clouded
> Cane conducts the dancers of Bali,
> The lesser celandine sprouts in Lagos.
>
> ('Old Masters Abroad')

His own cultural confrontations take place across centuries, in 'Dark Age Glosses': on Bede's image of the swallow in the barn; on Grettir and Njal's sagas, and the Four Masters' version of the battle of Clontarf. MacNeice is quite open in making his bridges between then and now in the first three poems, as in 'On the Grettir Saga': 'The burly major they denied / The Victoria Cross ... / ... for some reason reminds me / Of the strong man of Iceland ...'. Beneath such calculated resemblances gaps and continuities are revealed: Grettir and the major are doomed, but Grettir is also haunted, knew fear no man could induce; the bird's flight remains a potent symbol even to men unconfined to winter barns. The lesson drawn from Njal's saga, 'that even then, / ... Men had the nobler qualities of men', seems too pat a conclusion when contrasted with the subtler consideration of Clontarf. Here, because the place still exists, MacNeice could play with interpretations whose possible validity stands independent of his own: modern visitors, ancient historians, contemporary historians. 'The light was no doubt the same, the ecology different: / All Ireland drowned in woods.' The shift from 'ecology' to 'drowned' marks the two extremes: modern and factual, and the romantic past, into which MacNeice seeks to inject a little realism by recalling that destruction was as likely to be wrought by 'the monks' compatriots' as by the Norsemen. The poem's circularity, ending on 'The light was no doubt the same—and just as rich', makes amends for astringency, admitting that each might be persuaded by the gilding light into his varying conjectures.

The half-loving, half-willing belief, yet exasperated and disillusioned tone of the poem is MacNeice's now customary reaction to Ireland. *Solstices* contains many poems referring back to his childhood, although the memories rely less on nightmare and harshness than usual. 'Half Truth from Cape Town' elicits those qualities:

> When I was young and at home I could not tell
> What problems roosting ten miles to the west
> Waited like vultures in their gantried nest
> Till Prod should tumble Papish in the river.

But the speaking voice is adult, retrospective, it lacks the bitterness of 'Belfast' and the barely distanced terror of 'Auto-biography'. So in 'The Riddle', the child's 'clammy suspicion' that its answer was 'going round and round the house, evil, waiting to get me' (*Strings*, p. 38) does not surface because of the calm perspective in which the question is posed. The warmth of the kitchen range on small faces, the adult existential query, rob the cook's riddle of its original power.

'Country Week-end', described by MacNeice in the *Bulletin* as one of his 'deliberate exercises in simplicity or at least in a penny-plain technique', also evidences a cosier view of child-hood than had been admitted into the poems before. Mac-Neice was at this time establishing himself in Hertfordshire and left the BBC the next year to take up free-lance work, main-taining a programme contract with the Corporation for half a year. In gradually loosening his ties with London, he perhaps felt that he was embarking on a way of life closer to that which tempted him in rural Ireland, a way of recovering a more natural sense of time. The first section of the poem establishes constants of experience stretching back beyond memory; untypically, MacNeice does not dwell on how long he will be there to see them, or how long they will last. Real children are present, whose function is similar to the ghostly ones in *Burnt Norton*: they are gaiety, discovery, movement, continuity. The section's symbol is the circle; in the notebook draft he had thought of beginning the third stanza, 'Concentric circles: cups and plates'.[5] By choosing 'Outgoing heirlooms' he allows that the countryside may not survive, instead of emphasizing security, but 'outgoing' here also means 'going outwards', and the stanza expands from domesticity to infinity (to Larkin's 'unfenced existence' in fact, without the younger poet's endorse-ment of its superiority):

> Outgoing heirlooms; cups and plates,
> Nettle and colt's foot, elder hedge,
> Blackthorn beyond, then field on field,
> And then the skyline; then the sky.

The second section spans a smaller history, goes back to the War when MacNeice ferrets out a pair of hobnail boots. The relaxed indulgence of this poem is somewhat deceptive: the urban-dweller recognizes an element of make-believe in his week-ending, wants the earth to 'add weight to what I have read / And wish to think I feel'. The boots connect him to his own past, to a possible future, and to 'the world of folk-tales: / What third son setting forth to bilk an ogre / Or pluck a bride from her redoubt of thorn / Ever wore shoes?'

The sequence seems to be very loosely organized around the four elements: air in I, with sky and birdsong; earth in II and now water, light/fire dominating IV. MacNeice is washed back to days before the War:

> As if hypnotised, as if this wet
> Day were the sum and essence of days
> When such spinning shafts of steely water
> Struck to numb, or revive, the mind.

Altering the lines from their passive draft form and changing the adjective 'shining' to 'steely' gave this section a sharper edge, makes memory itself less indulgent, needling, and testing. When MacNeice wrote 'Much further back, in my childhood' (1), he took some of the immediacy from the experience of watching funerals. He restored it with 'Much further back, a child ...', and thus linked it more precisely with his echo from 1 Corinthians 13, seeing the graveside mourners 'Crossing the pane, through the rain darkly'. Not only is this an important and poignant vignette, it is also expressed compassionately: it comprehends the childish emotion while allowing for a potentially unchildlike acceptance of death in a different spirit. The mutability of lives is conveyed explicitly by the memories, implicitly by the rain itself. Water is almost always benedictory in MacNeice's poetry and so it proves at the end, combined with wind to encourage a new setting out.

'Country Week-end' bears more than one trace of Mac-Neice's reading of *Four Quartets*, as in the old theme of arrival as return in the fourth section, when the circle is drawn and the lighting of lamps establishes stability. 'We have been here a thousand years / Nor yet have reached the age of gas'; these lines from the first stanza of section I link the opening with the oil-lamps of section IV, a light making 'a different / Evening from those elsewhere', as MacNeice originally wrote (1); in changing it to '... from our usual' he touchingly makes of their company an old habit.[6] The night-lights of his childhood have previously thrown only the shadows of nightmare, but here candle-light is distinguished from the reassurance of the lamps carried by 'Bustling dead women with steady hands, / One from Tyrone and one from Cavan / And one my mother;' the identification has a Yeatsian cadence. This natural calm induces MacNeice to inveigh against technology as symbolized by the swtich, only a brief flicker though before he rounds off the poem, tongue-in-cheek: 'One good night in a naughty world'.[7]

Brisk 'Nature Notes' succeed 'Country Week-end', again dealing with his childhood which had been, according to these poems, brightened by dandelions, leavened by cats, bridged by corncrakes, rattled by the sea. Each is 'incorrigible' in its own way, the 'unsubtle' alternating with the 'subtle'. That Mac-Neice should choose 'incorrigible' as the key word, after having used it so memorably in 'Snow', indicates a freshened delight in unpredictable nature. The neatness of the sequence carries its own buoyancy, plucking each light string. MacNeice is not interested in the inherent nature of dandelions or corncrakes in the way Ted Hughes or Jon Silkin are when they describe a pike or a bluebell; the notes are half-comparisons with facets of human nature, flirtatious women, confident men. They are *jeux d'esprit*, as are the 'Sleeping Winds' and, in a drier tone, 'Indoor Sports'.

This renewed confidence which enables him to celebrate the tangible pleasures of childhood also encourages exploration of old fears, notably in 'The Blasphemies'. It bears resemblance to an unpublished poem of which there is only an undated draft extant, called 'Tipperary' (Texas), probably written in the 1950s, perhaps during the period of *Visitations*. 'The Blasphemies' is organized around the theme of belief, whereas 'Tipperary' is a chronological account of events in MacNeice's life, especially those influencing his poetry. He recounted how daytime activities, particularly writing, began to absorb him sufficiently for the night-time haunting to cease, 'except for an obsession with the Sin against the Holy Ghost'. Having discovered the sin to be saying 'Damn God', he could never resist saying the words in his mind, although he struggled against the urge to do so, 'and once you said that you were lost' (*Strings*, p. 59). 'The Blasphemies' opens with the nightly tussle: 'Damn anyone else, but once I—No, / That is the

unforgivable blasphemy.'⁸ Changing 'That is' to 'Here lies'
intensifies the sense of defiance which possesses the child, who
knows the consequences. MacNeice goes on in the autobiography to describe the background of his life, the War, and
it is this the first stanza of 'Tipperary' describes:

> From the papering of the nursery the time of Tipperary
>   He had come a long way,
> From the chasing of fritillaries & sticking flags in
>   war-maps,
> From the brash bells & bonfires on Armistice Day,
> From the forgetting of childhood pains, the learning
>   to be sly & wary,
>   He had come a long way.
>
> From the rich purple sulks & the glimmers of adolescence
>   There was yet a way to go,
> ~~From the shot silk of his early loves threaded with~~
>   ~~self-pity~~   ? ×
> From the doubts & the devils & the cock about to crow,
> From seventeen years of iron & bronze & stone-age
>   effervescence,   ?
>   A long way to go.

In 'Tipperary' MacNeice is more indulgent of his youth, or
at least his self-criticism is tempered with a certain affection for
the outward show; in 'The Blasphemies' the second stanza
reveals the bleakness behind the mocking exterior. The turn to
parody—here he no doubt remembered his 'I once had a dear
little God, dears, / So neatly and sweetly aloof' (Texas: c.1928)—
could not make nonsense of shibboleths because they were not
believed in the first instance: 'And what is a joke about God if
you do not / Accept His existence? Where is the blasphemy? /
No Hell at seventeen feels empty.' Rising thirty, humanism is
all, so grounds for blasphemy are lacking again: 'The only
failure was not to face / The facts.' The facts at thirty are
dismissed in 'The Blasphemies'; in the earlier poem they still
smart, and need three stanzas for their exorcism:

> From his so-called coming of age, from the search
>   for the Universal,
>   He had come a long way,

From that island of Calypso where no one could
  grow older,
From the flowers and the fetters of the torchlight play,
From the break-up on the raft, the storm & the dispersal
  He had come a long way.
         greed
        ~~lust~~
From the maze of ~~love~~ & guilt, from the attempt to
  be public-minded   ?
  There was yet a way to go,
From the spy glass on Madrid or Addis Ababa or
  Munich,
From the gradual dissolution of the mockery kings
  of snow,
               staring into the sun
From thirty years of ~~looking, looking again~~ & being
  blinded,
  A long way to go.
              that set
         passion setting fire to
From that tower of ice & ~~longing, dropping sparks~~
  ~~on~~ New York City
  He had come a long way,
        voice   out of a box
From that ~~box~~ letting 'Evil Things' ~~into a room~~ in
  neutral Dublin,   ?
From years which added up to one black night & one
  grey day,
           for which he felt he
From the carcase of a world on ~~which a vulture~~
  should feel
  ~~might have~~ pity
  He had come a long way.
From the pendulum swing to God, from professional
  complacence,
  There was yet a way to go.
        world-watching
From forty years ~~observing~~ from a seat back to the
  engine

> With both the world & himself snapping 'I told you
>   so',   × ?
>   love
> From the searching for a something to make ~~suit~~ to
>   or obeisance,
>   A long way to go.
>
> ~~&~~nagged at by the world's & his own I-Told-You-So
> ~~As he listened to the world's & his own 'I told you so'~~

This deep disillusionment and weariness has already been
remarked in the poems MacNeice wrote in his forties. He
judges the poetry specifically in 'The Blasphemies': his need is
presented in professional terms, whereas the swing of God had
appeared to answer more than that. Using the symbols familiar
to him from childhood is seen as mere word-play, insufficient
without belief, and no longer universally comprehended. Mac-
Neice had felt in the War a kinship with his community born of
circumstance, but in the 1950s the shared frame of reference
had dissolved. In this penultimate stanza his symbolism is
deliberately Christian but explicitly questioned:

> Have we not all of us been in a war
> So have we not carried call it a cross
> Which was never our fault? Yet how can a cross
> Be never your fault? The words of the myth,
> Now merely that and no longer faith,
> ~~Melt in his hands, hands which were never~~
> ~~Truly pierced, & he can no longer~~
>   which were never proved
> Hard as nails, nor can he longer
> Speak for the world—or himself—at forty.

The turning of the phrase about his hands avoids the indentifi-
cation he had just queried and relies on a colloquial simile,
although the religious connotation is inescapable.

    The two poems conclude on quite different notes. 'Tipperary'
returns to its opening image as though the previous scenes have
been dreams, excursions from childhood that always end back
there. The penultimate line plays on 'a way to go' as meaning
death, and his one positive claim does not alleviate the general
tone of slightly embittered discontent.

So with nearly fifty years of cancellation & frustration
   He has come a long way
   (Maybe yet a way to go)
And his self-examination has been both contrived &
   cursory
   While the men he made of snow
   Have consumed their fitful day,   daemonic
Yet he still can claim some moments of a ~~given~~
   illumination   × ?
While he waits for his old nurse to finish papering
   the nursery—
   Which is perhaps a way to go,
   Perhaps a long long way.[9]

'Daemonic illumination' recalls a poem written in 1937, published as 'Thank you' in *The Earth Compels*, as 'For Services Rendered' in *Poems* (1937), and as 'Daemonium' in *Poems 1925-1940*, in which the daemon celebrated is a fount of sensual awareness, of physical dexterity: 'Who skating on the lovely wafers of appearance / Have held my hand, put vetoes on my reason, / Sent me to look for berries in the proper season.' No such gaiety enters 'Tipperary' or 'The Blasphemies', but the latter does finish with an unassertive assurance, a tolerant curiosity that is an advance on his earlier humanism because it dismisses nothing out of hand. He is now 'a walking question'. The first weakly inclusive qualification, 'but not a cheap one, no more / Than anything else is cheap', has been tightened: '… but no more cheap than any / Question or quest is cheap'. This is a more self-accepting, less egotistical poem than the earlier one, although their basic structure is clearly similar. 'Tipperary' uses its model to generalize the experience and to distance it from its narrator, but the poise is not always successfully maintained. By the time he wrote 'The Blasphemies', perhaps only a few years later, MacNeice could be both frank and detached.

Sometimes his admissions could only be framed in 'contemplative parable' (see the Argo recording sleeve notes), and then they do become genuinely accessible types of experience: such a poem is 'The Truisms', about a generation's inheritance, abandoned and then unwittingly entered into. The symbol of the

unknown yet familiar house is a particularly potent one for
MacNeice, as in 'Order to View', where the sudden gust of wind
that brings things to life around and inside the house opens the
world. Here too, the spirit finds itself instinctively at ease, 'it
was where he had come from':

> He raised his hand and blessed his home;
> The truisms flew and perched on his shoulders
> And a tall tree sprouted from his father's grave.

If this circularity seems too easily reassuring, the same symbol as
used in 'Selva Oscura' is disquieting. MacNeice chose the poem
for his Argo recording to demonstrate that he was 'often back
with personal relationships but, I trust, with a deeper perspective and with less frills, less fever'.

> Perhaps suddenly too I strike a clearing and see
> Some unknown house—or was it mine?—but now
> It welcomes whom I miss in welcoming me;
> The door swings open and a hand
> Beckons to all the life my days allow.

The gravity and simplicity of the poem had not been within his
range for a long time: it looks effortless, not facile. The reference
to Dante via Eliot is lightly carried; its recognition is far from
essential although it increases appreciation of the personal
landscape that MacNeice constructs. Comparison with two
poems from 1946 having similar components confirms an
impression of new mastery. The third stanza of 'Selva Oscura'
closes: 'Or, finding bluebells bathe my feet, / Know that the
world, though more, is also I.' In 'Bluebells', MacNeice had
used the flower as a symbol of hope, of the rebirth of a marriage
strained by its resumption after the War. To explain their
precise significance, the woman is given a stanza to spell out
the analogy between blue flowers in a dark wood and her own
desire for a means of reconciliation. After the direct statement
of their plight, it is too mannered. Whereas in the later poem
meaning can be safely implied in a phrase, left flexible yet not
vague. 'Woods', an excellent poem not intended to convey the
darker meaning of 'Selva Oscura', is packed with illustration,
similes, overt literary references, and ends with a stanza of
description indulged in for sheer pleasure: it helps to gauge
how difficult the lesson was that MacNeice chose to learn.

'And I recognise even more than before that form is part of the content and that one of the most important formal activities is omission.' This comment on the Argo record sleeve echoes an earlier one, made in a review of George Seferis's *Poems*. 'It would be interesting ... to make an analytical comparison of Seferis and his Italian contemporary Salvatore Quasimodo, the title of one of whose poems, "A me pellegrino", might serve for so much of Seferis's work. In both of them the sense of absence seems to become something positive, (*New Statesman*, 17 December 1960, p. 978). MacNeice produced a programme on *The Poems of Salvatore Quasimodo* (broadcast 2 November 1961), for which he translated 'Dialogo', a more complex and rhetorical composition than 'A me pellegrino' but no doubt its use of the Orpheus myth appealed to him. 'A me pellegrino' indeed relies on absences for its charge: the returning traveller is no longer met by a welcoming voice, the square is abandoned, even the beauty conjured by light is illusory. Quasimodo juxtaposes this encounter with his past with a memory of the black-shawled women of his southern province, 'parlano a mezza voce della morte'. It is as though the sources of the poem were barely tapped; signs are given but there is no attempt at circumscription. Such reticence is extreme and fruitful. Mac-Neice would have been drawn by both poets' continual concern with themes of voyaging and exile, with explorations of blurred personal and racial histories.

He pointed to 'The Wall' among his own poems as an example of the attempt 'to write very simply and starkly' (record sleeve). The problem lay in finding the balance he achieved in 'Selva Oscura', so that the reader feels absence has resonance, is not simply a failure. 'The Wall' describes a transfiguration: wall to window, light, and intimations of a garden; it emerges as mere sleight-of-hand instead of profundity. The identification 'The first garden. The last' is also made in 'Apple Blossom', only turned around. In both poems there is the assertion that endings are beginnings, equally both lack the sense that this is an earned conviction, it looks more like a pleasant juggling with words. What MacNeice admired in Herbert, the conveyance of deeply felt truths in sometimes deliberately flat diction, eludes him.

On the other hand, 'Homage to Wren (a memory of 1941)'

demonstrates his ability to learn from Herbert, in its organic images, element of surprise, use of domestic detail. Whereas in the poems about London's bombing MacNeice had caught the spirit of Pepys, whom he had quoted in his 1941 broadcast on St. Paul's—'horrid malicious bloody flame'—, this is written with undiluted enjoyment, has a nursery-rhyme aura of watching danger from comfort, '... Sir Christopher Wren had made everything shipshape'. He can afford to celebrate the flames as they leap and curvet; and after strictly maintaining the correspondences ship/St. Paul's, sea/fire, he finishes his tour of duty with a natural gesture that in these circumstances springs its own surprise:

> I climbed to the crow's nest for one last look at the
> roaring foam,
> League upon league of scarlet and gold,
> But it was cold so I stretched out my hands from
> the drunken mast
> And warmed my hands at London and went home.

In the *Bulletin* note on *Solstices*, MacNeice concluded by saying that his position had been 'aptly expressed by the dying Mrs Gradgrind in Dickens's *Hard Times*: "I think there's a pain somewhere in the room but I couldn't positively say that I have got it." So, whether these recent poems should be labelled "personal" or "impersonal", I feel that somewhere in the room there is a pain—and also, I trust, an alleviation.' There is a marked recognition of the possibility of global catastrophe, as well as of lurking individual doom: 'Some one has got to pay for the round' ('Yours Next'); 'Neither sense nor conscience stirred, / Having been ultimately deterred' ('Jericho'); 'He turned and saw the accusing clock / Race like a torrent round a rock' ('The Slow Starter'). MacNeice rarely lends an 'I' to these perceptions: they are presented as overt/covert parables, using common turns of phrase, known situations, and giving them unfamiliar significance. His is not the 'making strange' technique, by which objects are lifted out of their usual context and in the new one are sharply redefined; MacNeice strips a familiar thing and puts it in such a light that its eeriness is revealed. This faculty was present in his earliest poetry, but there it could appear wilful, even a morbid distortion. The skill in this late volume lies in making the transformations unforced, answering to the logic of his imagination and persuading ours.

The process may be observed in two poems: 'Breaking Webs' (1928) and 'The Wiper' (c.1960). The first has a different subject for each of the first three stanzas, dwells on another in the next two, and returns in the sixth to the subject of the third, with sinister emphasis. Stanzas one, two, four, and five are connected by the theme of movement: 'The spider's belly-mind creates / Thoroughfare on thoroughfare'; 'The fatally inquisitive moth / ... Leaves its bed and board of cloth' and:

> Over asphalt, tar, and gravel
> My racing model happily purrs,
> Each charted road I yet unravel
> Out of my mind's six cylinders.
>
> Shutters of light, green and red,
> Slide up and down. Like mingled cries,
> Wind and sunlight clip and wed
> Behind the canopy of my eyes.

Against these is set the tapping of branches on a window-pane, which is at first merely wistful, then they grope 'After unseen fatalities'. MacNeice clearly wishes to create an aura of doom into which the inquiring or lively propel themselves unknowingly. In 'The Wiper', although his intention is somewhat similar, the treatment is sophisticated. The car-driver appears in every stanza but its centre is the road at night, an image for the monotony, mystery, isolation of life. Thus a much simpler set of integrated metaphors carries a complex perception. The car-ride in 'Breaking Webs' is the most striking of its images because least derivative, whereas the pessimistic omens are more contrived. MacNeice makes use of the same accessibility of experience in 'The Wiper', but the apparently inexorable pessimism of the journey itself is made to yeild its one consolation: the road,

> Which through the tiny segment
> Cleared and blurred by the wiper
> Is sucked in under the axle
>   To be spewed behind us and lost

> While we, dazzled by darkness,
> Haul the black future towards us
> Peeling the skin from our hands;
>   And yet we hold the road.

When writing this poem, MacNeice added in the *Bulletin*, he felt himself 'just as mythopoeic as if I were writing about the Grail (though I notice, to my own surprise, that *Solstices* contains practically no references to either Graeco-Roman or Christian legend)'. Allusions to a paradisal garden are perhaps more frequent than MacNeice himself realized: he is explicit in 'Idle Talk', which is partially intended as a defence of his poetic practice. Despite its being ill-used, casually and thoughtlessly employed, dense with banality, language unpredictably can be made to come alive, can be used in new perspectives which reveal true meaning, can be a flexible means of communicating the impossible. Adam to Eve:

> Looked and felt for the same three words
> Which he had uttered time and again
> But never like this, and said: 'I love you'.

This example in particular witnesses to MacNeice's old conviction that personal relationships, however uncertain, rewrite the world for us: 'Between the lines the words were strange / Yet not to be misunderstood', as he wrote in the exhilarated love poem 'Solstice'. 'Vistas' similarly offers the alleviation of love as rebirth, potential fulfilled. The sense of discovery is played out even in the form of 'All Over Again' where MacNeice omits punctuation entirely, runs on lines to reproduce the headiness of his emotion and its existence outside the constraints of time, flying in the face of likelihood. Yet he rhymes 'cliff' with 'if' at the beginning and end of the poem, knowing that supposition is dizzying, dangerous, the state itself only seemingly true.

These two poles of experience: being in love, completing a journey, being saved and, if that had not chanced, being alone, a confused transient, unable to help being lost, are staked out in the poems 'Good Dream' and 'Bad Dream'. When MacNeice explained in the opening Clark Lecture why he was attracted personally to parable writing, he gave as his first reason that he had 'from childhood been a steady dreamer (I mean in the literal sense)'. Before reading psychologists, he had already taken for granted that his dreams had their roots in his own real world, and he remembered 'in all periods of my life having dreams which had a fair degree of shape ... often akin to fairy stories' (*Parable*, p. 7). This accounts, at least in part, for the way he perceived the threat inherent in familiar objects. In 'Good Dream', there is the fairy-tale component of a journey across water to find the lost love on the other side: the whole dream has an accumulative magic and is given a dimension beyond that by MacNeice's use of biblical analogy, '*in the beginning / Is darkness upon the face of the earth*'. It is a dialogue in which the dream voice is the truth, socratically leading the dreamer to revelation. He 'hears / The ripples round the chair legs, hears / Larksong high in the chimney, hears / Rustling leaves in the wardrobe ...'. The room expands and becomes indivisible from the natural world, the dreamer awakes into a shared beatitude. The same domestic surrounding in 'Bad Dream' is utterly hideous, cankered by the intrusion of animals and insects: the hand reaching out to help becomes the hand pleading for help, which the dreamer cannot stir to grasp. It is a landscape of howling despair, and the dreamer is locked into it:

> Then everything buzzed and boomed. The chaps
>   outside on the lamp posts
> Hooted, broke wind, and wept,
> Men the size of flies dropped down his neck while
>   the mansized
> Flies gave just three cheers
> And he could not move. The darkness under the
>   floor gave just
> One shriek. The arm was gone.

While MacNeice's portrayal of joy has nearly always the same associations—'the gush / Of green, the stare of blue, the sieve / Of sun and shadow' ('Solstice')—his grimmer visions increase in power and range, marshal new images. Both kinds of poetry, and the lighter verse too, benefited from his more rigorous approach at the turn of the decade. *Visitations* shows MacNeice waiting for a sign, unwilling to impose one interpretation or form on his material, trying out sequences that

circle round a theme. With *Solstices* and *The   Burning Perch*
(1963) he has found his voice: most of the poems are taut,
concentrated; landscapes of dream and nightmare reach beyond
one man's experience, occasionally attain a mythical strength.
He achieved the balance in some that Eliot called in Catullus
'intense levity'. After appreciating in his early verse qualities
of spontaneity and casual brilliance, the late measured passion
takes us by surprise.

VI. FUNERAL GAMES

The Burning Perch was the Poetry Book Society's choice for autumn 1963, and MacNeice's comments on it for the *Bulletin* were among the last things he wrote. He admitted to being perplexed by the general sombreness of the collection, and uncertain as to the reason: 'Fear and resentment here seem to be serving me in the same way as Yeats in his old age claimed to be served by "lust and rage", and yet I had been equally fearful and resentful of the world we live in when I was writing *Solstices.*' Both Hedli MacNeice and Lady Nicholson have remarked in conversation on his fear of ageing: that he had to die disturbed him less than the prospect of slow decline, or the sight of elderly complacence. The circumstances of MacNeice's premature death in September 1963 were ironic. He had written a play, *Persons from Porlock*, about an artist who had failed to live up to his early promise and aspirations, and who blamed this failure on various distractions. The ultimate interruption the artist suffers is death, which he encounters while on a potholing expedition. Quite unnecessarily, MacNeice went underground with the BBC sound engineers to record effects for the play, and caught a chill that developed into pneumonia. Lady Nicholson recalled seeing him in an oxygen tent two nights before he died, 'looking triumphant then, as though he were winning the struggle'. Appropriately, in these late poems the insistence on themes of lost time, lost opportunity, degeneration and death is not morbid; it is a defiant confrontation, a recognition of facts lurking beneath many guises.

An edge of wit remains, as in the elegant 'Tree Party'; unserious in its nice rhymes and the formula of the toast, while continually courting the possibility of disaster. The salute to the pine was originally: 'Your health Master Pine, you stand in the snow / Needling away ...' (Texas). The change shows MacNeice's willingness at this time to avoid the easily punning connections which formerly he would have indulged. When the thirteenth stanza is reached, with the mention of the poet's own death (the opening stanza implied the eventual death of his

creative energies), it has the surprise and simplicity of lines
from Herbert. The rhyme gives a faintly mocking intonation:

> Your health, Master Yew. My bones are few
> And I fully admit my rent is due,
> But do not be vexed, I will postdate a cheque for you.

In a volume where two-thirds of the poems are about, or
marginally concerned with, dying, such chiding acceptance is
uniquely unresentful.

The greater power of this later poetry is demonstrated too in
the poems of place. The city-portraits are much more com-
pressed than 'Visit to Rouen', for instance, the contrasts less
obviously staged. 'Caught between Roman and Turk a dream
takes shape / And becomes Constant ...'; the slight alteration
of tone, a visionary possibility offered, prepares us for the last
lines of 'Constant' which go beyond the sum of historical
events. The sky:

> Red with repeated fires, accidental or designed,
> Sags like a tent over riot and ruin and one
> Who calmly, having other things in mind,
> Bears on his palm the Church of the Holy Wisdom.

The random end-rhyming here has the effect of tightening the
structure before the final line is set loose, its drifting length
enacting the unconcern of the saint. Constantinople bears
witness to different kinds of changelessness: a recurrently
ruinous history, the enduring image of Santa Sophia.

Egypt gave rise to two poems for *Visitations*, in which Mac-
Neice grappled with the inconceivable age of the Nile and its
civilization. Perhaps spurred by the Aswan Dam crisis, he
returned to the Pharaohs' tombs in 1961/2 as a subject of
apprehension, and cause in 'This is the Life' of satire, Roman
in its mockery. Whereas in 'The National Gallery' art was for
MacNeice a window on to 'a vital but changeless world— /
a day-dream free from doubt', in 'Réchauffé' art of an unfamiliar culture has infinite power to disturb.

MacNeice thought 'This is the Life' the nearest to pure
satire in *The Burning Perch*, but it seemed to him 'no more
purely satirical than, for example, a medieval gargoyle'
(*Bulletin*). His old penchant for using and subverting clichés

succeeds entirely, since he relies upon a well-defined frame of reference. His draft for the poem shows that after the first two lines he had an idea of how it should close: he jotted down '& Pharaoh's portion of turkey and pumpkin pie', lightly deleted it, continued with what are printed as the eighth and ninth lines, then the sixth and seventh and the conclusion (Texas). This shorter version lacked the description that fleshes out the title, and the sense of burrowing descent. It did have the lines beginning 'Gracious in granite' with that phrase's exactly appropriate House-and-Garden air. The eventual organization of the poem is masterly, ten long lines of eight stresses forming one sentence. Stephen Wall, in his generally rather disparaging review of *The Burning Perch*, calls the poem 'excellently professional' and justly remarks that it 'swims free of its creator' (*Review*, July 1964, p. 94).

The 'deep peace' offered by the tombs is that of the fall-out shelter: even more than in *Solstices*, the possibility of a global catastrophe haunts MacNeice, shadowing poem after poem. Newspaper events no longer impinge directly on his work, but an atmosphere of crisis profoundly affects it. The threat is not merely personal, nor is its form precise, thus its repercussions are unconfined. Nature itself is thrown out of gear. In 'Spring Cleaning' MacNeice abandons his usual, if qualified, optimism about the season, drops any suggestion that it might bring renewal. As in 'Bagpipe Music', the reader is pelted with a heterogeneous collection of objects and situations. For all the futility of the gestures described in the earlier poem, the verse itself has a harsh gaiety, a reeling measure; while each wish or act may be ultimately useless against the impending crash, they are temporarily seductive. The poem written in 1961 barely holds out against the centrifugal tendency of the world it depicts. Sentences are staccato and tenuously connected. This is not the midwinter spring presaging discovery, it is an unholy, sterile confusion:

> Blain and dazzle together, together
> Magnolia in bloom and holly in berry
> In the writing desk where nothing is written
> Lurk latchkeys, counterfoils and lockets.

The denial of continuity is contained even in these hidden objects.

Three poems in succession come to the same deadly halt: 'Spring Cleaning', 'Another Cold May', 'The Pale Panther'. The second of these returns to the chess metaphor of 'Solitary Travel' (*Solstices*), elaborating it throughout the poem; everything moves not of its own volition but time's. 'The tulips tug at their roots and mourn / In inaudible frequencies': these windblown flowers are strikingly different from some MacNeice described in 'The Policeman', an undergraduate paper he gave at Corpus Christi: 'No one knows what the soul is like who has not seen a flower drunken, tousled, flushed, and swaying, tugging and swearing at its stalk and trying to break away and failing' (*Strings*, p. 274). Excitement has drained away, boredom and horror have set in. 'The Pale Panther' combines the tone and phrasing of thirties' poetry— '... burns / Whose gift is not to cure'; 'As for you, airman, ...'—with the savagery to which MacNeice was aroused by the renewed threat of apocalypse.

He felt that boredom impinged strongly on 'October in Bloomsbury', where it shades into leisurely indifference. In previous poems about the neighbourhood, centring on the British Museum, MacNeice had conceded some power to the statues and books, or had implied that value lay in the simple fact of being sentient in those surroundings. His last poem remains undisturbed by anything after the Edwardians, including the less sedate of the phrases it contains, neutralizing any signs of vivacity or of doom. The affront to time which the sculptures constitute is only possible for artefacts: the living, nearly always taken by surprise (as in 'Birthright'), must resentfully submit.

MacNeice had always proposed love as a way of sidestepping temporality, or at least of successfully disregarding it. In 'Déjà Vu' the old defiance is shown, but a certain weariness is also evident, and 'The green improbable fields' of the dedicatory poem are perhaps only half believed in. Clearest of all is the statement made by 'The Introduction'. The potential lovers meet at the wrong time in their lives, and the green of nature indicates corruption rather than rebirth; instead of becoming butterflies, 'the larvae / Split themselves laughing'. The 'grave glade' of the opening line, evocative of romance (as in Robert Weever's poem, 'In a harbour greene ...', which MacNeice liked to quote), already hints at the closing transmutation:

The string quartet in the back of the mind
Was all tuned up with nowhere to go.
They were introduced in a green grave.

A sense of alternatives slithering from his grasp is given autobiographical expression in 'Star-gazer', 'Memoranda to Horace', and 'Goodbye to London'.

Possibly the memory of a particular 'brilliant starry night' surfaced at this point because MacNeice had been commissioned to put together a book on astrology, which was published post-humously. Despite his discernible intention, 'Star-gazer' remains curiously unrefined, as though he lost the impetus to convert a childhood memory thoroughly into poetry. It is noticeably casual beside the balanced art of the following poem.

'Goodbye to London', judging by the Berg draft, seems to have been written with the same ease as 'Star-gazer'; while the latter is rhymed yet relaxed in syntax, the former has a flatness of diction relieved by the formal, rhyming refrain. MacNeice took the last line from Dunbar's poem 'In Honour of the City of London', also in seven stanzas, with its refrain 'London thou art the flour of cities all'. Dunbar has only praise to offer, comparing the city to flowers and jewels—'jasper of jocunditie / Most myghty carbuncle of vertue and valour'—and to Troy, rejoicing in the life of river and street, The whole has the dense-packed brilliance of medieval miniatures. When MacNeice calls it 'the great mean city' in the opening line, he sets the tone of his poem: 'great' here indicates both size and quality; although 'mean' is pejorative, it hints at the opposite sense, as in Paul's declaration that he was 'a citizen of no mean city' Acts 21:39). Such ambiguity of judgement persists, rein-forced by the refrain acknowledging that London has been a flower, though its petals are now falling. As in 'October in Bloomsbury', MacNeice is not confident that absence will enable him to be entirely detached from old haunts.

He had long been divided in his reaction to city life. When he connected London with love, it became marvellously exciting and sensuous, so also when it was endangered. 'Trilogy for X', written in the summer of 1938, is a compelling instance:

March gave clear days,
  Gave unaccustomed sunshine,
Prelude to who knows
  What dead end or downfall;
O my love, to
  Browse in the painted prelude.

Regent's Park was
  Gay with ducks and deck-chairs,
Omens were absent,
  Cooks bought cloves and parsley;
O my love, to
  Stop one's ears to omens.   (III)

'Christmas Shopping', on the other hand, portrays the com-
mercially harried citizens: '... through the tubes of London /
The dead winds blow the crowds like beasts in flight from / Fire
in the forest'. Connolly remarked in 'Lianas Over the Void'
that MacNeice's 'real preoccupation was with everyday life in
bohemian London', and quoted from *Autumn Journal*, 'A smell
of French bread in Charlotte Street' (Canto V). The bombing
of the city put an end to these notations of daily life, and description centred on buildings under fire rather than people or
his own London round. *Autumn Sequel* blends real London with
myth, so that Regent's Park exists only briefly in its own right
before becoming a type of Eden. All these strands, stretching
from the earliest astonishment—'and never in the world had
there been so much so quickly' (*Strings*, p. 63)—to the late
disillusionment, were to be tied off. MacNeice separated some
for counting in the poem.

  After expressing his intention and describing London's
assault on a child's ears and nostrils, MacNeice turns to his
'peering teens' to evoke the sophistication he then discerned.
The fourth stanza, showing him at ease in the city, had one
change in the draft: 'Later as a place to work in and love in';
the substitution of 'live' for 'work' matches the jaunty familiarity
of the whole, an overlapping of worlds. When it comes to the
War, MacNeice's sentiments are clear, apart from a slight
difficulty with the first line of stanza six ('From which reborn
into anticlimax'); it is downhill all the way and the final refrain

makes a causal connection: the 'meaningless buildings' and renewed estrangement of the Londoners are the reason 'why now the petals fall / Fast from the flower of cities all'. The failure of community, definitive and ugly isolation, bear witness to human inadequacies resurgent after the extraordinary demands made by war were lifted. MacNeice backs away from the scene more in sadness than in resignation.

MacNeice's moving tribute to Horace, the radio programme *Carpe Diem* (broadcast 8 October 1956), opens with lines that could serve as an epigraph for 'Goodbye to London' or 'Memoranda to Horace': 'fastidiosam desere copiam ...' (*Odes*, III. 29), interpreted as: 'Say goodbye to arrogant luxury and to the towering buildings that reach the clouds and cease to admire the smoke and riches and the racket of wealthy London [Rome]'. Characterizing the period *entre deux guerres*, Quintus, the protagonist, quotes from Horace's seventh ode (Book I):

> o fortes peioraque passi
> mecum saepe viri, nunc vino pellite curas;
> cras ingens iterabimus aequor

which he translates:

> O my brave comrades, who with me have suffered
> worse things often, now dispel your cares with wine.
>
> Cras—tomorrow: ingens—the huge: iterabimus—we shall repeat, have another slap at: aequor—the sea. And whatever the sea stands for.

This anticipates the theme of some of *The Burning Perch* poems; 'Round the Corner', for example, and 'Thalassa', and the lines to which Quintus turns next are directly quoted in 'Memoranda to Horace': 'lusisti satis, edisti satis atque bibisti: / tempus abire tibi est ...', which he renders: 'You have played enough, you have eaten enough and drunk enough. It is time for you to depart' (*Epistles* 2:2).

Carpe Diem is clearly the product of a mind which felt deep affinities with Horace's poetry and the attitudes it revealed, nevertheless MacNeice was aware of their differences, and chose to argue out the matter some years later. Formally, there is a conscious attempt to suggest Horatian rhythms (in English of course one cannot do more than suggest them) combined with the merest reminiscence of Horatian syntax. ... I suppose it goes with something of a Horatian resignation. But my resignation, as I was not brought up a pagan, is more of a fraud than Horace's: *Memoranda to Horace* itself, I hope, shows this. (*Bulletin*)

From boyhood MacNeice had admired the glitter of Horace— 'O fons Bandusiae splendidior vitro' (III.13)—and 'his tidiness, realising that English with its articles and lack of inflexions could hardly ever equal Horace either in concentration or in subtlety of word-order' (*Modern Poetry*, p. 49). In 'Memoranda' he does suggest the alcaic metre, and adopt some Horatian habits: the dry, sometimes prosaic diction, sentences spread over several stanzas, anaphora. He does not follow Horace in the occasional separation of adjectives from their nouns, though a similar effect of suspension is achieved in section III: 'And another called it "intense" but admiringly "levity"'. The conversational tone has something of Horace's urbanity, of his public moralizing also, an assumption of shared and civilized values. Those had been expressed in MacNeice's description of the ideal poet in *Modern Poetry* and of the ideal life in Canto XII of *Autumn Journal*, and Auden perhaps bore them in mind when he provided the MacNeice entry for the Gotham Book Mart's twentieth anniversary catalogue, 'We Are the Moderns' (New York, 1939): 'Ireland gave him a love of the gracefully individual, the odd amusing detail, the disorderly charming; Latin and Greek a linguistic discipline and a distrust of vagueness in expression. ... He is perhaps the only poet today whose work is directly in the classical tradition. Both as a person and as an artist, the first descriptive adjective he suggests to one is "Elegant", and the first writer of whom one is reminded is Horace ...'. Section IV of 'Memoranda' indicates the ground on which MacNeice and Horace meet as poets: 'an appetitive decorum', more Apollonian than Dionysian, that is tending to stress, rather than obliterate, distinctions; 'The point is never to recognize / Any preconception: let commonplace be novelty.' That the integrity of this poetic—and personal—stance is threatened from all directions provokes from MacNeice a desperately bleak response, distant from both the resignation and alleviation Horace offers.

The prospect of 'a second childhood remembering only /
Childhood' affords scant consolation in 'Memoranda', in part
because MacNeice's attitude was not that of a writer who, in
re-enacting childhood experience, could rediscover his faith in
innocence and vision. In his poetry at least, recollection proceeds from an adult perspective, the chasm between then and
now is always visible, although a bridge may be slung across it.
Apart from the brief mention in 'Memoranda', MacNeice left
his Irish childhood behind in *The Burning Perch*, preferring to
deal with it in prose. He did tinker with a poem about changing
homes, using the longer lines with which he latterly tried to
sidestep 'the "iambic" groove which we were all born into'
(*Bulletin*):

> We never, when I was a child, moved house, it was
>   always the Rectory
> Though the town encroached and the corncrakes
>   left but when I left too
> My father was translated south to a walled garden
>   and a rookery
> And portraits of earlier bishops ...
>
> (Texas, *c.*1961)

The poem continues with a play on the linguistic rather than
ecclesiastical associations of translation, and tails off in a description of familiar photographs trying to acclimatize themselves
to change, 'cricking their necks / In the strange rooms'. This
has a certain charm, but its lack of incisiveness makes it un-
typical of MacNeice's poetry in the 1960s. It is interesting to
see him abandoning a poem which relies for its impetus on the
sort of word-play he might have found adequate to its support
a few years before.

The three last collections have in common an increasing
patience with the material, a willingness to drop an attractive
solution for something less facile. Drafts for *The Burning Perch*
show that although MacNeice might frequently think of a near
cliché or tag, he was more rigorous at this stage than previously,
and mindful of his weaknesses. On the other hand, the one-
stanza long-lined poems, which look as if they have been poured
out with barely a hesitation, in fact read this way in draft. Particularly in poems for his final volume, MacNeice often seems

to have known at the outset how he wanted a poem to end, and this clarity of thought ensures spareness and control without in any way confining the poems' power. Material is rarely discarded, and in that respect there is a return to his early practice, but whereas MacNeice's youthful poetry was inclusive because everything seemed to him inherently interesting, the last poems do not require pruning because of the initial sureness of their conception. True to his own critical insistence, form and content here go hand in hand. The change in one parallels the alteration in the other: from the reliance on things seen, smelled, touched, to provide a starting-point, to the growing concentration on states of being whose meaning could only be approached by symbols.

MacNeice's bent at this time, indeed for some time past, was towards myth, allegory, fairy-tale, the modes of writing he characterized as 'parable' in the Clark Lectures. His love of fairy-tales was long-established, documented in *Modern Poetry* as well as *Varieties of Parable*. Anthony Blunt, recalling their reading at Marlborough, mentions that 'on the completely fancy side—and this went with the cult of the childlike and childish we all had—we read Edward Lear, Lord Dunsany's fairy stories and Grimm; Andersen we thought rather smug and we preferred Grim as being more vivid' ('From Bloomsbury to Marxism', p. 164). MacNeice's later preference was for Andersen, whom he praises in *Varieties of Parable* for the spiritual quality of his quests and his lack of sentimentality. Grimm, and Dunsany in another way, satisfied a craving for the baroque and fantastic, elements whose excess eventually lost appeal for MacNeice. When he was nineteen, he could still identify with a book by Dunsany, albeit half-seriously: 'I am having a golfing holiday with the curate as a result of *The Charwoman's Shadow* where the magician decides boar hunting to be the surest way to happiness and the best philosophy. It's a good book and the last chapter—"The End of the Golden Age"—is just like me only refined.'[1] Dunsany is charmingly archaic, a little dusty, a tapestry-maker. There is not a hint of modernity, or much of humour, nor is there a strong moral sense. The magician skilled in black arts closes the book with his disappearance from earth into a community beyond the grave, neither heaven nor hell. John Hilton, in his contribution to the

Radio Portrait, suggested that MacNeice's having 'preoccupied himself so much with fables and legends and myths, and abstract thought and visual sensations, and poetry of course' meant that he encountered the world with more of a shock than most people, but also with 'an extraordinary freshness of vision' (p. 6). By the 1960s, unsurprisingly, almost the reverse of this movement was taking place, a return to parable in which Mac-Neice could utilize his sharp contemporary observations, meshing this world with that of legend. When the fabulous and the everyday interact in his late work, it is rarely in the benign sense of 'Good Dream', and is usually a cause for unease or dread. His interest in the quest, never dormant since his discovery of the *Morte d'Arthur*, and an increasing fascination with death, could not be served by a dazzling style, which would only conceal and soften. A deep admiration for Bunyan and Herbert emerges from *Varieties of Parable*. Their method of revelation is plainness: 'the knife that almost killed the writer will cut the reader to the bone' (p. 23).

Obviously the result of MacNeice's preoccupations bore no resemblance to the ornate poetry of *Blind Fireworks*—'I was in those days only too happy mixing up Greek, biblical and Nordic [mythology]' ('Images', p. 129)—nor much to the carefully constructed myths of *Autumn Sequel*. He was aware that ' "things have come to such a pass that we do not even recognise great numbers of symbols" belonging to our tradition, which is half Judaic-Christian and half Graeco-Roman'; he was conscious of the pitfalls of employing private systems.[2] Yet others were no longer widely comprehensible to a writer's audience because of 'the destruction of the rigid base of authority upon which allegory traditionally depends'.[3] Yet it was possible to draw from classical, medieval, and folk traditions those recurrent patterns and images which remained valid. Undoubtedly the experience of adapting and writing for radio alerted MacNeice to their potential.

This vein of writing was formally and metaphysically challenging: the dilemmas are most clearly posed by the work for radio. In 1949, when MacNeice previewed his play *The Queen of Air and Darkness*, he claimed that 'rather than trying to write a morality, I have been trying to write a myth', in which fleshed-out characters would carry the allegorical burden; in

1962 he admitted *The Mad Islands* to be 'another attempt to write a modern morality'.[4] The problem in writing allegorical drama, MacNeice found, was that tragedy and the concepts of good and evil edged their way in; he compared his difficulties to those facing George MacDonald in *Lilith*. 'But my superstructure was less convincing than MacDonald's', he confessed, 'because I lacked his groundwork of belief' (*Parable*, p. 112). The interplay between belief and artefact caused MacNeice intermittent anxiety throughout his life. In *Modern Poetry* he owned to feeling 'hampered by this lack of belief or system' when he went up to Oxford; part of his optimism about contemporary poetry arose from the fact that beliefs were increasing among poets, which 'should conduce to a wider, more fertile and possibly a major poetry', although he emphasized that '*for the poet*, any belief, any creed ... should be compromised with his own individual observation' (pp. 62, 101). Apropos of Dante, MacNeice made the point in his first Clark Lecture that while in poetry 'the formal elements are part of the meaning or the content', the content (which includes beliefs) will naturally 'have a part in the shaping of that poem. Which means that in this respect the beliefs are formalising elements' (*Parable*, p. 19). MacNeice knew why he had failed outright in *The Queen*, and the reason for his return to *Everyman* as a dramatic model is also explained by remarks in the second Lecture. 'It moves forward inexorably from beginning to end and there are no ambiguities. ... Its virtues are the prose virtues of Bunyan, ... [the style] is spare and undecorated and sometimes colloquial' (*Parable*). While MacNeice did not ignore psychological intricacies, the structure of his moralities is quite plain: the protagonists move towards their deaths, and at some stage they recognize the direction they are taking. The shape is dictated by the summing-up of a life. Many of *The Burning Perch* poems are also cast in this mould.

In his lecture 'Contemporary Poetry and Drama', MacNeice quoted Beckett as having said 'I am interested in the shape of ideas even if I do not believe in them', and continued: 'Now a playwright, like a poet, being a maker (or 'makar') is thereby *ipso facto* a shaper ... and this very act of shaping may bring him back full circle into something very like belief ...'.[5] The script MacNeice wrote for the CBS series 'What I Believe' (Texas:

dated *c*.November 1952) reveals a circularity in his thinking. This public avowal did not evoke deep consideration from MacNeice, but he eventually answered: 'What I do believe is that, as a human being, it is my duty to make patterns and to contribute to order—good patterns and good order.' Ten years later he might have answered differently, however the idea of pattern still seems central to his thought. How 'good' is to be defined—aesthetically or morally—is left unsaid. MacNeice's unwillingness or inability to define it could only be a weakness when he came to writing avowed moralities.

The compass of a poem was better suited to his strengths; implications could be left inexact, as in 'The Taxis', whose very simplicity is disquieting. The parable/poem partakes of 'the nightmarish world of the drunk or of the haunted', Mac-Neice wrote in an uncharacteristic note on a typescript (Texas). His observation in *Zoo* that 'the taxi represents Escape' (p. 125) indicates some of the poem's irony, since the passenger's past is riding with him. The nuances are particularly delicate: the placing of 'tra-la' in the four stanzas for instance, insouciant at first, knowing in the second, automatic in the third, and by the fourth wearied. 'The cabby looked / Through him and said: ...' is a nice stroke, conveying incidentally the driver's disgruntlement as well as the passenger's joining the insubstantial company. Technically the poem is beautifully finished, but its meaning is not circumscribed, gingerly balanced between this world and another.

McKinnon draws attention to the comment of MacNeice's Sherborne English master that he should 'avoid G. K. Chesterton and slang in writing' and quotes a passage from Chesterton's essays *The Uses of Diversity* concerning the image of strangers who become companions on a journey: 'That profound feeling of mortal fraternity and frailty, which tells us we are indeed all in the same boat, is not the less true if expressed in the formula that we are all in the same bus' (McKinnon, p. 71). If MacNeice had read and recalled this, it was not in Chesterton's genial, consolatory way that he perceived the metaphor. He used it in 'Figure of Eight' (*Visitations*), 'Hold-Up' (*Solstices*), and in an unpublished poem 'The Move', probably written in 1961 (Texas).

These three attempts are eclipsed by 'Charon' (1962), one of

MacNeice's most powerful poems. His initial idea for it exists in draft, with the first and last lines which remained unaltered.

The conductor's hands were black with money

Charon

If you want to die, you will have to pay for it.

with so many people aggressively vacant
pigeons & rumours of wars

When we reached the Thames
All the bridges were down.

A community of anxiety and doom exists on the journey. Tricks of repetition suit the narrative voice, which manages to be both incredulous and matter-of-fact, noting significance with hindsight. It has some of the London motifs of *Autumn Journal*: pigeons, wars, cock-crow; and 'that dissolving map' is a thirtyish property. The transition to the ferryman reveals both how bleak MacNeice's vision of ordinary life had become, and how much more sophisticated his craft, that Styx and Thames could now merge. He clearly had made the connection at once between the London bus conductor's grimy hands and those of Charon, who traditionally demanded an obol from his passengers; the Greeks used to bury the dead with the coin in their mouths. His age, labour, and distance from the beauty of Hellenic statues is economically, chillingly conveyed. MacNeice's narrative assurance makes the poem's progress inevitable, its ending inescapable. Whether this is a warning from someone who has paid and gone over, or the terrible memory of someone who could not pay but knows what will, some time, take place again, we cannot tell. The flatness of the closing statement is an example of that sleight-of-hand writing MacNeice spoke of admiringly in *Varieties of Parable*: it promises an end yet it goes on reverberating:

... We flicked the flashlight
And there was the ferryman, just as Virgil
And Dante had seen him. He looked at us coldly
And his eyes were dead and his hands on the oar
Were black with obols and varicose veins
Marbled his calves and he said to us coldly:
If you want to die you will have to pay for it.

Charon, who in the *Inferno* is grim and violent, with flashing eyes and a quick tongue, is terrible here because of the sheer lack of passion in his transaction with those on the bank. Mac-Neice could bring to the established myth his peculiar sense of the way something domestic or routine can be an ambush.

In the *Bulletin* MacNeice commented that most of the poems in *The Burning Perch* 'are two-way affairs or at least spiral ones: even in the most evil picture the good things, like the sea ... are still there around the corner'. This perception had its childhood basis, which MacNeice recounts in 'Landscapes of Childhood and Youth': '... round a corner I ran head on into a yet tangier surprise, one which is with me still when the open sea catches me unawares' (*Strings*, p. 218; cf. p. 87 above). It was also borne out in his reading of Seferis's poems:

> We knew it that the islands were beautiful
> Somewhere roundabout here where we are groping,
> Maybe a little lower or a little higher,
> No distance away at all.
>
> (from *Mythistorema*, No. 8)

MacNeice added in his review: 'Which perhaps *is* an answer; on a plane just a shade above or below our own or just around the corner which after all is our own corner, so near and yet so far in fact, lies something which might make sense of both our past and future and so redeem our present.'[6]

The sea as the plane of self-discovery dominates MacNeice's radio play *The Mad Islands*, written the following year (broadcast 4 April 1962). It is based on the Celtic legend of the Irish Voyages. Like Tennyson in his 'Voyage of Maeldune', Mac-Neice used some of the thirty-one original islands and invented others for the series of fantastic visits paid by Muldoon in the course of his quest. He acknowledged a debt to Alwyn and Brinley Rees's *Celtic Heritage*, also used in the Clark Lectures, where he quoted their remark that 'boundaries between territories, like boundaries between years and between seasons, are lines along which the supernatural intrudes through the surface of existence' (*Parable*, p. 100). It is just this sense of worlds intersecting that he captures in the encounters of the seafarer with the islands.

Where water meets the land is always potent territory for

MacNeice's imagination: the scene of childhood memories, of particular associations with his father, the passage between his two allegiances, England and Ireland. Drawing attention to Auden's book *The Enchafèd Flood*, MacNeice pointed out that the Romantic attitude to the sea, which we have inherited, is *'dialectical*: the sea, Auden says, is "the Alpha of existence, the symbol of potentiality", but it also remains what the ancients thought it, the first and last symbol of primeval chaos, of the indefatigable destroyer' (*Parable*, p. 84). The sea is symbolic of escape and freedom but also of exile, and in Horace's poetry, a metaphor for 'eternal exile'.

Thus it is appropriate that the last of MacNeice's *Collected Poems*, which was not published in *The Burning Perch* and appeared posthumously in *The London Magazine*, should be 'Thalassa'.[7] Daring the surge, knowing the history of such attempts, MacNeice holds courage as an absolute value. The poem gathers resonance from centuries of literary precedent, has an almost Tennysonian ring. He ended *The Burning Perch* with a just conceivable prospect, 'when the tunnels meet beneath the mountain', recalling the fantastic landscape of a MacDonald novel, or the symbolism of his own *Prisoner's Progress*. The *Collected Poems* finishes by breaking out of that enclosed world, balancing pessimism with a steadiness that has taken into account the worst and is still capable of affirmation. MacNeice himself escapes his poetic limitations, is triumphant.

> Butting through scarps of moving marble
> The narwhal dares us to be free;
> By a high star our course is set.
> Our end is Life. Put out to sea.

MacNeice quoted in his book on Yeats a reminder from the poet's father: 'It should never be forgotten that poetry is the Voice of the Solitary Spirit, prose the language of the sociable-minded' (*Yeats*, p. 38). He himself seems to have been divided between these extremes: the mercurial, gay, enchanting, witty companion of whom his close friends have spoken, who almost always surfaces in the vivid prose; argumentative, as ready to watch a rugby match as to write, conscious of his ancestry in the nation of great talkers. And the aloof, solitary, uncommuni-cative spirit, burdened by memory, bruised by exile, ready to

love and expecting to be abandoned; intensely aware of ephem-
erality and unable to console himself with his father's belief, or
any other. Out of this conflict issued his poetry, which he considered in any case a Jekyll and Hyde affair, and in his own
collaboration 'it is mostly Hyde—self-pity, greed, nostalgia'
(*Minch*, p. 176). It was informed by decent, humanist values:
such values combined with a troubled sense of their short-
comings have belonged to fine poets, but not to the great ones
without some leavening intuition of transcendent powers. He
had not that supreme confidence and the necessary degree of
self-absorption to use poetry explicitly as his quest, conducting
a public dialogue with himself. A pervasive scepticism prevented
that, just as MacNeice's natural inclination to be engaged with
what he was communicating ruled out a classical objectivity.
Things were important because he saw or experienced them
and the act of his doing so stamped their verbal formulation.
'But the things that happen to one often seem better than the
things one chooses. Even in writing poetry, ... the few poems
or passages which I find wear well have something of accident
about them ...' (*Strings*, p. 220).

If MacNeice is not in the company of Yeats and Eliot, among
modern poets, his achievement is still considerable. Most of his
poems indicate the limits within which they operate: as the
drafts show, MacNeice rarely surprised himself by a perception,
did not stretch himself beyond his capacities. But these were
technically impressive from the beginning; equally striking was
his sensuous apprehension, which gave everyday objects and
events an unsuspected resonance, combined with irony and
a knowledge of the bleaker patches of life. MacNeice was dedicated to being a professional poet, one of the Makers; he eventually learnt, through a period of deep discouragement and
effort, to temper the kind of writing that came easily to him
with the demanding art of opening his poems to imponderable
forces, tapping reserves of dream, parable, and myth.

NOTES

CHAPTER I

1. Elizabeth Nicholson, 'Trees Were Green', in *Time Was Away*, ed. Terence Brown and Alec Reid (Dublin: Dolmen Press, 1974), p. 14.
2. *The Strings are False* (London: Faber and Faber, 1965), p. 75.
3. *The Poetry of W. B. Yeats* (London: OUP, 1941; paperback edition, 1967), p. 52.
4. *Strings*, p. 78.
5. 'Experiences with Images', in *Orpheus*, vol. 2, ed. John Lehmann (London: John Lehmann, 1949), p. 129.
6. Littleton Powys, *The Joy of It* (London: Chapman and Hall, 1937), p. 61.
7. *Radio Portrait of Louis MacNeice*, narr. Goronwy Rees, 7 September 1966. Transcription, p. 2.
8. Minutes of the Marlborough Lower Sixth Literary Society, 13 June 1926.
9. This and subsequent relevant quotations are from: 'Eliot and the Adolescent', in *T. S. Eliot, a symposium*, ed. Richard Marsh and Tambimuttu (London: Editions Poetry, 1948), pp. 146-51.
10. E. R. Dodds, *Missing Persons*, (Oxford: Clarendon Press, 1977), p. 117.
11. 'Images', p. 129.
12. Ibid., p. 128.
13. Ibid., p. 130.
14. *Yeats*, p. 191.
15. Ibid., p. 156.
16. 'Under the Sugar Loaf', *New Statesman*, 29 June 1962, p. 948.
17. *Radio Portrait*, p. 8.
18. 'Louis MacNeice', in *Responsibilities of the Critic*, ed. John Rackcliffe (New York: OUP, 1952), pp. 107-8.
19. *Zoo* (London: Michael Joseph Ltd., 1938), pp. 84, 79.
20. The second line occurs more appropriately in 'A Serene Evening': 'The garden to-night is all Renoir and Keats, / In the mouth melting to forgetfulness'. Self-quotation is frequent in *Blind Fireworks*.
21. *Strings*, p. 53.
22. 'Wounds', Michael Longley.
23. *I Crossed the Minch* (London: Longmans, Green and Co., 1938), p. 155.
24. *Missing Persons*, pp. 117-18.
25. 'Images', p. 128.
26. *The Auden Generation* (London: Bodley Head, 1976), p. 187.

CHAPTER II

1. (Oxford: Basil Blackwell, 1927), p.v.
2. 'Poetry To-day', in *The Arts To-day*, ed. Geoffrey Grigson (London: John Lane, 1935), p. 44.
3. Ibid., pp. 56-7.
4. Ibid., p. 66.
5. 'Psychology and Art To-day', ibid., p. 20.
6. 'Subject in Modern Poetry', *Essays and Studies*, 22 (1937), p. 149.
7. Ibid., p. 156.
8. Letter to Blunt, postmarked 3 February 1934. Misc. 37F. Gollancz had rejected this second volume after the failure of *Blind Fireworks*: 834 copies remaindered out of a run of 1,000. Sheila Hodges quotes the reader's report: 'The collision of a Sitwell with an Alousian [sic—Aldousian?] strain has here produced a telescoping of pregnant similes in most admired confusion of echolalic cadences. The process often strikes out brilliant images, but it is too caviare, I feel, for your list.' *Gollancz: The Story of a Publishing House 1928-1978* (London: Victor Gollancz Ltd., 1978), p. 73.
9. *Strings*, p. 146.
10. *Pastoral Poetry and Pastoral Drama* (London: A. H. Bullen, 1906), p. 7.
11. Anthony Blunt, 'From Bloomsbury to Marxism', *Studio International*, November 1973, p. 165; subsequent quotations, pp. 166, 167, 168.
12. November 1937, p. 11.
13. 'The pause before the film again / Bursts in a shower of golden rain.' Bergonzi suggests that MacNeice is alluding deliberately to Zeus's appearance to the Danae: 'The film could manifest a godlike power and the cinema was a temple as well as a picture palace.' *Reading the Thirties* (London: Macmillan, 1978), p. 126.
14. Letter to Blunt, postmarked 27 March 1927. Misc. 37B.
15. Dodds describes in *Missing Persons* Stephen MacKenna's 'heroic struggle' to edit Plotinus (p. 63). While he was compiling a life and letters of Mac-Kenna, MacNeice joined him in Dublin; the trip included a sedate tea with Yeats.
16. *The Auden Generation*, p. 291.
17. *TLS*, 7 August 1937, p. 572.
18. Letter to Blunt, 7 May 1936. Misc. 37G; see also *Strings*, p. 157.
19. The Humanities Research Centre at Texas has a bound set of *New Verse* with annotations and letters received by the editor.
20. *Louis MacNeice Reading His Own Poems*, Argo, RG196.
21. *Apollo's Blended Dream* (London: OUP, 1971), p. 203.
22. 'Letter to W. H. Auden', *New Verse*, November 1937, p. 12.
23. *Responsibilities*, p. 108.
24. Letter to Blunt, postmarked 8 June 1934. Misc. 37F.
25. Letter to Eliot, 9 May [1936].
26. Letter to Doone, 22 July [1935], Berg; text of the 'Dialogue' published as *Group Theatre Paper*, No. 6, Berg; 'The Play and the Audience', in *Footnotes to the Theatre*, ed. R. D. Charques (London: Peter Davies, 1938), pp.32-43.
27. This and subsequent information from *Missing Persons*, p. 132.

28. 'From that Island', Autumn 1939, pp. 468-71. Jarrell also pointed out, with some acerbity, that the title actually meant modern English poetry, since MacNeice took no account of Wallace Stevens or William Carlos Williams, for example, and made only fleeting mention of Pound.
29. Cyril Connolly, *Radio Portrait*, Columbia transcription, n.p. The transcriptions held in the Rare Book and Manuscript Library, Columbia University (New York) are unedited versions of the contributions, and will be indicated henceforth as C.t.
30. 'The *Faust* Translation', in *Time Was Away*, p. 70.
31. *New Writing in Europe* (Harmondsworth: Allen Lane, Penguin Books, 1940), p. 116.
32. Baudelaire quoted by MacNeice in his review of Cocteau's *Infernal Machine*, *London Mercury*, February/April 1937, p. 430; Schwartz, 'Adroitly Naïve', *Poetry* (Chicago), May 1936, pp. 115-17.
33. Surely Larkin, who in his obituary notice for MacNeice (*New Statesman*, 6 September 1963, p. 294) admired the 'brilliantly quotidian reportage of *Autumn Journal*', recalled this passage when writing 'The Whitsun Weddings'.
34. MacNeice's thanks

... that the ranks
   Of men are ranks of men, no more of cyphers.
So that if now alone
   I must pursue this life, it will not be only
A drag from numbered stone to numbered stone
   But a ladder of angels, river turning tidal.

perhaps owe something to a recollection of Francis Thompson's 'In No Strange Land': 'The angels keep their ancient places; — / Turn but a stone and start a wing!'; '... upon thy so sore loss/ Shall shine the traffic of Jacob's ladder / Pitched betwixt Heaven and Charing Cross'.
35. '... oddly it might seem, in view of my romantic disposition, I was beginning to prefer Aristotle to Plato ... For all his famous dryness, Aristotle... never let transcendental radiance destroy the shapes of creatures or impose a white-out on everything.' 'When I Was Twenty-One', in *The Saturday Book 21*, ed. John Hadfield (London: Hutchinson, 1961), pp. 237-8.
36. 10 January 1939, p. 84.

CHAPTER III

1. 'Images', p. 130.
2. 'The Leaning Tower', in *Collected Essays*, vol. 2 (London: Hogarth Press, 1966), p. 172.
3. Cf. Empson's comment in the *Radio Portrait*: 'After the end of the war, the poets nearly all said how bitterly ashamed they felt for having turned out so dreadfully wrong, and said that now they weren't left-wing any more ... But Louis at any rate never appeared in a white gown as a penitent; he went on being sardonic and responsible, hardly surprised even when appalled.' (p. 12).

4. Letter to Dodds from Belfast, 24 September 1939.

5. *Horizon,* February 1940, p. 68.

6. As quoted by Robin Skelton in the introduction to his anthology *Poetry of the Forties* (Harmondsworth: Penguin Books Ltd., 1968), p. 17.

7. *Strings*, p. 210. See p. 210 ff. for an account of this Irish visit which complements the sequence originally called 'The Coming of War', later 'The Closing Album'.

8. *Strings*, p. 30 ff.

9. Letter to Dodds, 22 November 1939. Of these poems, thirteen were published: three were never collected, and of the ten that were printed in *Poems 1925-1940* under the title 'Octets', only four were retained in the *Collected Poems* (1949 and 1966), collectively titled 'Entered in the Minutes'.

10. 'Are There Any Rules?', *Well Versed*, 8; broadcast 13 June 1941.

11. Quoted by Eric Homberger, *The Art of the Real* (London: J. M. Dent and Sons Ltd., 1977), p. 43.

12. Ronald Blythe in his introduction to *Components of the Scene* (Harmondsworth: Penguin Books Ltd., 1966), p. 14.

13. 'John Keats' in *Fifteen Poets* (Oxford: Clarendon Press, 1941), p. 354.

14. In his London letter, MacNeice wrote about the heart-break of seeing disemboweled houses in the East End, and his contrary exhilaration observing damage done to the great West End emporiums: '... the whole street is tinkling as the shop-walkers stand in their windows and sweep the glass on to the pavement where luxury objects lie scattered among torn-up flagstones and drunken lamp-posts; ... first of all it is the building that is on fire, but later it is the fire that is the solid object, the building is just a gim-crack screen that the fire has folded around itself.' July 1941, pp. 206-7.

15.   Lascio lo fele, e vo per dolci pomi
             promessi a me per lo verace duca;
             ma infino al centro pria convien ch'i tomi.

        '... I am leaving the gall and going on for the sweet fruits promised me by my truthful Leader; but first I must go down to the centre.'

                                                        Inferno, XVI, 61 ff.

16. *The Revenant* (Dublin: the Cuala Press, 1975), introduction by Hedli MacNeice, p. 7. The *Collected Poems* contains the last lyric, 'The nearness of remoteness like a lion's eye', p. 199.

CHAPTER IV

1. *The Bell,* October 1947, p. 69.

2. MacNeice excepted the Apocalyptics. Predictably, he did not care for their extreme romanticism: 'This group of poets compares badly with their predecessor on Patmos.' 'An Alphabet of Literary Prejudices', *The Windmill*, 9, 1948, p. 38.

3. *Poetry of the Present* (London: Phoenix House Ltd., 1949), pp. 18, 21, 22.

4. *Strings*, p. 99. The refrain of 'Alisoun' runs: 'An hendy hap ichabbe y-hent, / Ichot from hevene it is me sent, / From alle wymmen my love is lent / Ant lyht on Alisoun.'

5. 'The Sideliner', *New Statesman*, 4 April 1953, p. 402. See also 'Notes on the Way', *Time and Tide*, 28 June 1952, pp. 709-10.

6. Roy Craven, *A Concise History of Indian Art* (London: Thames and Hudson, 1976), p. 148.

7. 'English Poetry Today', *The Listener*, 2 September 1948, p. 346.

8. 'A Poet of our Time', 28 October 1949, p. 696. The reviewer was a Dr Cox, probably the R. G. Cox who used to review for *Scrutiny*, which was generally hostile towards MacNeice.

9. Quoted by MacNeice in his review of it and *Mavericks*, 'Lost Generations?', *London Magazine*, April 1957, p. 52.

10. Letter to Mrs Borden Stevenson, 31 March 1953. Texas.

11. 'Four British Poets', Summer 1953, pp. 473-6.

12. 'Lianas Over the Void', a review of the *Collected Poems, Sunday Times*, 15 January 1967, p. 28.

13. Dan Davin, 'In a Green Grave', *Closing Times* (London: OUP, 1975), p. 55.

14. 'To my present taste this sort of economy—the *twist* of an ordinary phrase, the apparently flat statement with a double meaning—is far more exciting than the romantic elaboration of glamour images' ('Images', p. 132).

CHAPTER V

1. 'He Weeps by the Side of the Ocean', *New Statesman*, 5 December 1953, p. 721.

2. *Varieties of Parable* (Cambridge University Press, 1965), p. 9.

3. Broadcast respectively: 9 November 1952, 27 April 1954, 25 July 1959. Only the folk-tale was published, in *Persons from Porlock and Other Plays for Radio* (London: BBC, 1969).

4. Rosamund Tuve, *A Reading of George Herbert*, reviewed in the *New Statesman*, 13 September 1952, pp. 293-4; Margaret Bottrall, *George Herbert*, and Joseph H. Summers, *George Herbert*, reviewed in the *London Magazine*, August 1954, pp. 74-7.

5. Texas: BBC notebook draft (1).

6. This accords with the spirit of the volume's closing lyric, 'All Over Again': 'As if I had known you for years ...'.

7. The evocation of serenity is similar to that in a very early poem, 'Evening Indoors'. The closing lines play on Portia's words to Nerissa, on seeing the lights of her house: 'So shines a good deed in a naughty world'. *The Merchant of Venice*, v. i.

8. Texas: typed manuscript with autograph emendations.

9. 'The Snow Man' (*Solstices*) also uses the image for a crumbling past, but it contains the possibility that the thaw is not simply destruction: 'Or is it rather a dance of water / To replace, relive, that dance of white?'

CHAPTER VI

1. Letter to Blunt, postmarked 25 September 1926. Misc. 37A.

2. Quotation from Tuve's *A Reading of George Herbert* in his review of the book, op. cit.

3. Edwin Honig, *The Dark Conceit,* quoted in *Parable,* p. 28.

4. ' "Listeners are Warned ..." a study in Evil', *Radio Times,* 25 March 1949, p. 10; programme note, *Radio Times*, 29 March 1962, p. 39.

5. *Parable,* p. 118. Cf. his point that while astrological determinism could be pushed to excess, the concept of universal 'correspondances' is attractive: 'This grouping of interrelated creatures and objects has the same appeal as certain card games with their sequences, flushes and so on. It all goes back to the basic concept of *sympathy* ...'. It draws 'the mystic in us. And there is an equally strong attraction for the poet in us, or at any rate for the pattern-maker.' *Astrology* (London: Aldus Books in association with W. H. Allen, 1964), pp. 16-17.

6. 'A Modern Odyssey', op. cit. See also Brown, p. 121, who draws the two comments together and links them with the poem 'Round the Corner'.

7. February 1964, p. 5. It may have been sketched years before. Texas holds a typed carbon-copy contents list for *Springboard,* with autograph additions and deletions, which includes the title 'Run Out the Boat', dated January 1944. On another contents list for the volume, the title 'Run Out the Boat' is inserted between 'Prayer Before Birth' and 'Brother Fire', then deleted, with 'Thalassa' substituted. Unfortunately, there are no corresponding manuscripts.

NOTES ON MANUSCRIPTS

Letters from MacNeice were made available to me by Faber and Faber and Lady Nicholson; those belonging to Professor Dodds and John Hilton have now been deposited in the Bodleian Library. I have also quoted from those given by Professor Blunt to King's College Library, Cambridge. Radio programmes were read in either the Play Library or the Script Library of the BBC.

The unpublished poetry and prose, and the drafts, are to be found in five collections:

1. The MacNeice Estate. I have cited from three manuscripts in Mrs Mac-Neice's possession: a typescript article entitled 'Broken Windows / Thinking Aloud'; a large holograph notebook containing mostly fair copies of poems dating from summer 1929, closing with an unpublished poem, 'Aeroplane', dated May 1934; a similar notebook beginning with the 'Eclogue by a Five-barred Gate' (May 1934) and ending with a deleted poem, 'The songs of jazz have told us ...', dated June 1936. In the text these are referred to as the 1929-34 Notebook, and the 1934-6 Notebook.

2. The Berg Collection, New York Public Library. The MacNeice section consists of plays and radio scripts; prose, including seven notebooks with outlines for a series of lectures given in Cape Town in 1959; and a selection of poetry manuscripts, many of which record only the final version of a poem, although some have interesting emendations. There are four notebooks with drafts for *Visitations*. The most extensive record of composition is provided by the manuscripts for *Autumn Sequel*, approximately two hundred and sixty pages in all. The Berg Collection also has letters and postcards from MacNeice to Rupert Doone, together with an interesting archive concerning the Group Theatre.

3. The Poetry/Rare Book Collection of the University Libraries, State University of New York at Buffalo. This too contains poems in their final versions, but has a few typed manuscripts with autograph corrections of interest. There is a small octavo BBC notebook with miscellaneous notes, including drafts of five poems for *Solstices*. Unfortunately the pencil writing has become so badly blurred that it is difficult to decipher. The other two notebooks are valuable. One, which I have called the 'spiral notebook', has drafts for eleven poems written in 1940, among them the ballades. The second, identified as the 'blue-covered notebook', has diaries of MacNeice's trips to Spain and Iceland, some of the poems for *Letters from Iceland*, and various deleted or unfinished drafts.

4. The Louis MacNeice Collection, Rare Book and Manuscript Library, Columbia University, New York. This small collection includes drafts of ten late poems, the unedited transcripts of contributions to the *Radio Portrait*, and thirty-eight books from MacNeice's library.

5. The Humanities Research Centre, University of Texas at Austin. There are letters to and from MacNeice, and the largest single collection of his manuscripts, between five and six hundred items. Again many of the manuscripts can be discounted as they do not differ from printed versions

of the poems, but the notebooks and pages excerpted from them contain numerous interesting drafts, including one hundred and fifty-three pages of material for *Ten Burnt Offerings*.

I have not thought it useful to append a complete bibliographical listing and description of the holdings; apart from the letters in King's College, few manuscripts have identifying numbers.

Papers in all the collections are well-preserved: the problem they present arises from MacNeice's habit of drafting in pencil, which has often smudged over the years and become illegible. His handwriting is generally not difficult to decipher; Grigson has characterized it as angular, 'rather like Gerard Manley Hopkins's hand' (*Radio Portrait*, p. 8).

SELECTIVE BIBLIOGRAPHY

1. BOOKS BY LOUIS MACNEICE

Blind Fireworks	London: Victor Gollancz, 1929
Roundabout Way (under the pseudonym Louis Malone)	London: Putnam, 1932
Poems	London: Faber and Faber, 1935
The Agamemnon of Aeschylus	London: Faber and Faber, 1936
Out of the Picture	London: Faber and Faber, 1937
Letters from Iceland (with W. H. Auden)	London: Faber and Faber, 1937
Poems	New York: Random House, 1937
The Earth Compels	London: Faber and Faber, 1938
I Crossed the Minch	London: Longmans, Green and Co., 1938
Modern Poetry: a Personal Essay	Oxford: OUP, 1938
Zoo	London: Michael Joseph, 1938
Autumn Journal	London: Faber and Faber, 1939
Selected Poems	London: Faber and Faber, 1940
The Last Ditch	Dublin: Cuala Press, 1940
Poems 1925-1940	New York: Random House, 1941
The Poetry of W. B. Yeats	London: OUP, 1941
Plant and Phantom	London: Faber and Faber, 1941
Christopher Columbus	London: Faber and Faber, 1944
Springboard	London: Faber and Faber, 1944
The Dark Tower and Other Radio Scrips	London: Faber and Faber, 1947
Holes in the Sky	London: Faber and Faber, 1948
Collected Poems 1925-1948	London: Faber and Faber, 1949
Goethe's Faust	London: Faber and Faber, 1951
Ten Burnt Offerings	London: Faber and Faber, 1952
Autumn Sequel	London: Faber and Faber, 1954
Visitations	London: Faber and Faber, 1957
Eighty-Five Poems Selected by the author	London: Faber and Faber, 1959
Solstices	London: Faber and Faber, 1961
The Burning Perch	London: Faber and Faber, 1963
The Mad Islands and The Administrator	London: Faber and Faber, 1964
Astrology	London: Aldus Books in association with W. H. Allen, 1964
Selected Poems Selected and Introduced by W. H. Auden	London: Faber and Faber, 1964
The Strings Are False: an Unfinished Autobiography with an appendix by John Hilton	Edited by E. R. Dodds. London: Faber and Faber, 1965

Varieties of Parable	Cambridge University Press, 1965
Collected Poems of Louis MacNeice	Edited by E. R. Dodds.
	London: Faber and Faber, 1966
One for the Grave: a modern	London: Faber and Faber, 1968
morality play	
Persons from Porlock and Other	Introduction by W. H. Auden.
Plays for Radio	London: BBC, 1969
The Revenant: a Song Cycle	Introduction by Hedli MacNeice
	Dublin: Cuala Press, 1975

2. CONTRIBUTIONS TO BOOKS AND PERIODICALS

'Poetry To-day'. In *The Arts To-day* Ed. Geoffrey Grigson. London: John Lane, Bodley Head, 1935, pp. 25-67.

'Sir Thomas Malory'. In *English Novelists: a survey of the novel by twenty contemporary novelists* Ed. Derek Verschoyle. London: Chatto and Windus, 1936, pp. 19-28.

'Subject in Modern Poetry'. In *Essays and Studies* by Members of the English Association. Oxford: Clarendon Press, 1937, pp. 144-58.

'The Hebrides: a tripper's commentary'. *The Listener*, 6 October 1937, pp. 718-20.

'Letter to W. H. Auden'. *New Verse*, November 1937, pp. 11-13.

'The Play and the Audience'. In *Footnotes to the Theatre*. Ed. R. D. Charques. London: Peter Davies, 1938, pp. 32-43.

'A Statement' (about political commitment). *New Verse*, Autumn 1938, p. 7.

'Original Sin'. Rev. of *The Family Reunion* by T. S. Eliot. *New Republic*, 3 May 1939, pp. 384-5.

'American Letter'. *Horizon*, July 1940, p. 462.

'John Keats'. In *Fifteen Poets*. Oxford: Clarendon Press, 1941, pp. 351-4.

'Traveller's Return'. *Horizon*, February 1941, pp. 110-17.

'London Letter'. *Common Sense*, February 1941, pp. 46-7.

'The Way We Live Now'. *Penguin New Writing*, 5, April 1941, pp. 9-15.

'London Letter'. *Common Sense*, April 1941, pp. 110-11.

'The Tower That Once', 'Stylite', 'Casualty of War (New York)'. In *Folios of New Writing*. Ed. John Lehman. London: Hogarth Press, Spring 1941, pp. 37-41, 147-8.

'London Letter'. *Common Sense*, May 1941, pp. 142-3. June 1941, pp. 174-5. July 1941, pp. 206-7.

'L'écrivain brittanique et la guerre'. *France libre*, December 1945, pp. 103-9.

'Eliot and the Adolescent'. In *T. S. Eliot, a symposium.* Compiled by Richard Marsh and Tambimuttu. London: Editions Poetry, 1948, pp. 146-51.

'An Alphabet of Literary Prejudices'. *Windmill*, 9, 1948, pp. 38-42.

'Experiences with Images'. In *Orpheus*, vol. 2. Ed. John Lehmann. London: John Lehmann, 1949, pp. 124-32.

'The Crash Landing'. *Botteghe Oscure*, 4, 1949, pp. 378-85.
'Listeners Are Warned...a Study in Evil'. *Radio Times*, 25 March 1949, p. 10.
'Poetry, the Public and the Critic'. *New Statesman*, 8 October 1949, pp. 380-1.
'Notes on the Way'. *Time and Tide*, 28 June 1952, pp. 709-10.
Rev. of *A Reading of George Herbert* by Rosamund Tuve. *New Statesman*, 13 September 1952, pp. 293-4.
'The Sideliner'. Rev. of Edward Lear's *Indian Journals*. *New Statesman*, 4 April 1953, p. 402.
Rev. of *George Herbert* by Margaret Bottrall and *George Herbert* by Joseph H. Summers. *London Magazine*, August 1954, pp. 74-6.
'Lost Generations?'. Rev. of *Poetry Now*, ed. G. S. Fraser and *Mavericks*, eds. Howard Sergeant and Dannie Abse. *London Magazine*, April 1957, pp. 52-5.
'Visitations' (note on volume). *Poetry Book Society Bulletin*, May 1957, p. 1.
'A Modern Odyssey'. Rev. of George Seferis's *Poems*, translated by Rex Warner. *New Statesman*, 17 December 1960, pp. 978-9.
'When I Was Twenty-One'. In *The Saturday Book 21*. Ed. John Hadfield. London: Hutchinson, 1961, pp. 230-9.
'Solstices' (note on volume). *Poetry Book Society Bulletin*, February 1961, p. 2.
'Under the Sugar Loaf'. *New Statesman*, 29 June 1962, p. 948.
'The Burning Perch' (note on volume). *Poetry Book Society Bulletin*, September 1963, p. 1.
'Childhood Memories'. *The Listener*, 12 December 1963, p. 990.
'Louis MacNeice in the Marlburian' (a reprint of some of his contributions, with an editorial note by John Hilton). *The Marlburian*, Michaelmas Term 1975, pp. 49-64.

3. ITEMS ABOUT LOUIS MACNEICE

ALVAREZ, A. Rev. of *Eighty-Five Poems. The Observer*, 8 March 1959, p. 23.

ARMITAGE, C. M., and NEIL CLARK *A Bibliography of the Works of Louis MacNeice* (with substantial omissions and some errors). London: Kaye and Ward, 1973.

AUDEN, W. H. 'The Cave of Making'. *The Listener*, 1 October 1964, p. 525; *About the House*, London: Faber and Faber, 1966, pp. 18-23.

BETJEMAN, JOHN 'Louis MacNeice and Bernard Spencer'. *London Magazine*, December 1963, pp. 62-4.

BISHOP, JOHN PEALE 'The Hamlet of Louis MacNeice'. Rev. of *Autumn Journal. The Nation*, 11 May 1940, pp. 602-4.

BLUNT, ANTHONY 'From Bloomsbury to Marxism'. *Studio International*, November 1973, pp. 164-8.

BROOKS, CLEANTH Rev. of *The Poetry of W. B. Yeats. Modern Language Notes*, April 1943, pp. 319-20.

BROWN, TERENCE *Louis MacNeice: Sceptical Vision*. Dublin: Gill and Macmillan, 1975.

BROWN, TERENCE, and ALEC REID, eds. — *Time Was Away: the World of Louis MacNeice*. Dublin: Dolmen Press, 1974.

CONNOLLY, CYRIL — 'Louis MacNeice in Middle Age'. Rev. of *Solstices*. *Sunday Times*, 12 March 1961, p. 31.

—— 'Lianas Over the Void'. Rev. of *Collected Poems*. *Sunday Times*, 15 January 1967, p. 28.

COULTON, BARBARA — *Louis MacNeice in the BBC*. London: Faber and Faber, 1980.

DAVIN, DAN — *Closing Times*. London: OUP, 1975.

DODDS, E. R. — *Missing Persons: an Autobiography*. Oxford: Clarendon Press, 1977.

ELIOT, T. S. — Letter. *The Times*, 5 September 1963, p. 14.

GARDINER, MARGARET — 'Louis MacNeice Remembered'. *Quarto*, May 1980, pp. 13-15.

GRIGSON, GEOFFREY — Rev. of *Poems* (1935). *The Criterion*, vol. xv, January 1936, pp. 320-3.

—— ed. *Poetry of the Present: an anthology of the thirties and after*. London: Phoenix House, 1949.

—— 'Black Orpheus'. Rev. of *Parable, Strings; Louis MacNeice* by John Press. *The Guardian*, 12 November 1965, p. 8.

GUNN, THOM — 'Modes of Control'. *Yale Review*, March 1964, pp. 447-58.

HEWISON, ROBERT — *Under Seige: Literary Life in London 1939-45*. London: Weidenfeld and Nicolson, 1977.

HOMBERGER, ERIC — *The Art of the Real: Poetry in England and America Since 1939*. London: J. M. Dent and Sons, 1977.

HYNES, SAMUEL — *The Auden Generation: Literature and Politics in England in the 1930s*. London: Bodley Head, 1976.

IREMONGER, VALENTIN — Rev. of *The Dark Tower*. *The Bell*, October 1947, pp. 67-70.

IRWIN, J. T. — 'MacNeice, Auden and the Art Ballad'. *Contemporary Literature*, Winter 1970, pp. 58-79.

JARRELL, RANDALL — 'From That Island'. Rev. of *Modern Poetry*. *Kenyon Review*, Autumn 1939, pp. 468-71. Reprinted in *Kipling, Auden & Co*. Manchester: Carcanet New Press Ltd, 1981, pp. 29-32.

LARKIN, PHILIP — 'Louis MacNeice'. *New Statesman*, 6 September 1963, p. 294.

LONGLEY, MICHAEL — 'The Neolithic Night: a note on the Irishness of Louis MacNeice'. In *Two Decades of Irish Writing*, ed. Douglas Dunn. Manchester: Carcanet New Press Ltd, 1975, pp. 98-104.

MATTHIESSEN, F. O. — 'Louis MacNeice', 'Yeats: the crooked road'. In *Responsibilities of the Critic*, ed. John Rackliffe. New York: OUP, 1952, pp. 25-40, 106-11.

McKINNON, WILLIAM T. — *Apollo's Blended Dream: a Study of the Poetry of Louis MacNeice*. London: OUP, 1971.

MERWIN, W. S. 'Four British Poets'. Rev. of *The Burnt Offering* [sic]. *Kenyon Review*, Summer 1953, pp. 461-76.

MOORE, D. B. *The Poetry of Louis MacNeice*. Leicester: the University Press, 1972.

PAULIN, TOM 'The Poetry of Displacement'. Rev. of *Collected Poems*. *Poetry Review*, March 1980, pp. 52-56.

—— 'The warm burrow of the BBC'. Rev. of *Louis MacNeice in the BBC*. *TLS*, 16 May 1980, p. 547.

POCOCK, ROBERT 'The Burning Perch'. *Encounter*, November 1969, pp. 70-4.

PRITCHETT, V. S. 'Bog Asphodel'. Rev. of *Parable, Strings*. *New Statesman*, 3 December 1965, pp. 886, 888.

PROCHASKA, ALICE *Young Writers of the Thirties*. National Portrait Gallery Exhibition Catalogue, London, 1976.

RODGERS, W. R. 'Tribute to Louis MacNeice'. *Ireland*, 30 September ǀ1963, pp. 4-5.

—— *Collected Poems*. With an introductory memoir by Dan Davin. London: OUP, 1971.

SCHWARTZ, DELMORE 'Adroitly Naïve'. Rev. of *Poems* (1935). Poetry (Chicago), May 1936, pp. 115-17.

SPENDER, STEPHEN 'MacNeice: Poet of the Passing Show'. Rev. of *Sceptical Vision*. *Books and Bookmen*, August 1975, pp. 20-2.

—— *The Thirties and After: Poetry, Politics, People (1933-75)*. London: Fontana/Collins, 1978.

Times Literary Supplement

—— 'Poetry'. Rev. of *Blind Fireworks*, 28 March 1929, p. 263.

—— 'Three Stages in Modern Poetry: the escape from private meanings'. Rev. of *The Earth Compels*, 7 May 1938, p. 314.

—— 'Poet's Apologia'. Rev. of *Modern Poetry*, 10 December 1938, p. 782.

—— 'A Poet's Moods'. Rev. of *Plant and Phantom*, 19 April 1941, p. 194.

—— 'A Poet in a Changing World'. Rev. of *Holes in the Sky*, 5 June 1948, p. 315.

—— 'A Poet of Our Time'. Rev. of *Collected Poems 1925-1948*, 28 October 1949, p. 696.

—— 'Mr MacNeice's Poems'. Rev. of *Ten Burnt Offerings*, 8 August 1952, p. 510.

—— 'The Poetry of Consciousness'. Rev. of *Autumn Sequel*, 26 November 1954, p. 754.

—— 'Poems of Maturity'. Rev. of *Visitations*, 7 June 1957, p. 350.

—— 'A Pattern of Poems'. Rev. of *Eighty-Five Poems*, 27 February 1959, p. 114.

—— 'Life in the Moment'. Rev. of *Solstices*, 31 March 1961, p. 199.

SELECTIVE BIBLIOGRAPHY

166

—— 'For Whom the Stars Look Up'. Rev. of *Parable, Strings*. 3 February 1966, p. 81.

THWAITE, ANTHONY 'Funeral Games'. Rev. of *The Poetry of Louis MacNeice* by D. B. Moore and *Apollo's Blended Dream* by William McKinnon. *New Statesman*, 10 March 1972, pp. 313-14.

WAIN, JOHN 'MacNeice as Critic'. *Encounter*, November 1966, pp. 49-55.

WALL, STEPHEN 'Louis MacNeice and the Line of Least Resistance'. *The Review*, 11-12, 1964, pp. 91-4.

WOOLF, VIRGINIA 'The Leaning Tower'. In *Collected Essays*, vol. 2. London: Hogarth Press, 1966, pp. 162-81.

INDEX